New Immigrants:

Portraits in Passage

New Immigrants:

Portraits in Passage

Thomas Bentz

The Pilgrim Press
New York

Library of Congress Cataloging in Publications Data

Bentz, Thomas, 1943-
    New immigrants, portraits in passage.

    1. Minorities—United States. 2. United States— Emigration and
immigration—Biography. 3. United States—Emigration and immigration. I. Title.
E184.A1B38   304.8'73   81-5160
ISBN 0-8298-0457-9 (pbk.)   AACR2

The Pilgrim Press, 132 West 31 Street, New York, New York 10001

to my parents
who make everyone feel
at home

Acknowledging all those who took me into their homes and hearts and brought this portrait gallery to life would fill these pages. Yet let me offer a few thank yous. For guidance and information: Maria Fiallo, Bettye Wiggs, Victor Azios, Manuel de la Rosa, Frank Galvan, Jorge Morales, Paul Ryoo, Jonathan Kim, Matthew Fong, Bienvenido Junasa, Daniel Romero, Roy Sano, Emau Petaia, Ralph Watkins, Steven Forester, Teruo Kawata, Mineo Katagiri, Nina Solarz, Sila Unutoa, Richard Wong. For translation: Minerva Antuna, Bruce Bliatout, Maria de Lourdes Porrata, Lillian Ayala, Alison McClure. For hospitality: Harold and Carmen Young-blood, Larry and Ki Henderson, James and Nancy Fredette, Doris and Oliver Thurman, Ford Coffman, Thomas Brown. For initial definition and overall support: David Rohlfing. For steady patience and ready aid while I lived like an alien: my wife Ellen.

Contents

	Preface	ix
	Introduction	xiii
Prologue	A Nation in Motion	xvii
Chapter 1	Feliciano y Diaz: Happy Days in Miami	1
Chapter 2	Gerard Jean-Juste: Stranger in Miami	33
Chapter 3	Maria de la Luz Romero: On the Border	63
Chapter 4	Jim Lockwood: Border Patrol	81
Chapter 5	Joe Razo: Sweatshop Sleuth	91
Chapter 6	Adriana: In the House of Torture	105
Chapter 7	David Won: Combat in Boston	119
Chapter 8	Wood Chuen Kwong: Canton to Chinatown	127
Chapter 9	Hoa Ky Luu: My Tho to San Francisco	137
Chapter 10	Loan Vo Le: Gem of Diamond Head	145
Chapter 11	Somsy Kuamtou: Lao in Kalihi	157
Chapter 12	Filipinas Amodo Sales: Molave on Brown Legs	163
Chapter 13	Sukie Uputuu Pouafe Abel: Samoa Meets Missouri	177
Afterword	Projection: Insurmountable Opportunities	185
	Appendixes	197
	Acknowledgments	209

Preface

At this very moment we as a nation are in the process of seriously reexamining our immigration policy. Calls for reform of the laws and regulations governing admission of immigrants and refugees have come from all sides, and the forum for reevaluation of our present policies has been the Select Commission on Immigration and Refugee Policy. As Chairman of that Commission, I have been privileged to hear from individuals, groups and public officials throughout our country who have an interest in our immigration policies. I have sensed that, while many Americans feel a need to achieve greater control over immigration, they also accept and continually reaffirm our national commitment to provide refuge, liberty and opportunity for those in the world still "yearning to breathe free."

Could we but know the entire story of those in our own families who left other lands to journey to America, we would recognize it retold in the pages that follow, differing perhaps in geographic or political detail, but consisting of very similar, and very human, hopes and fears, agonies and joys.

We often look back with pride to what our own ancestors

accomplished, not realizing that many of them also fled hunger and poverty, prison and oppression, to arrive destitute in a foreign land. Some came as exiles, indentured servants, and slaves—not by their own choice. Others worked for years to send family members to a new land of opportunity where they could earn enough to send for their families—perhaps one at a time. They brought with them the dreams of the new world and the customs of the old which, adapted to the conditions they found, became the fabric of America.

Those who seek our shores today are not different. They may come from different places on the globe, but their reasons for coming are strikingly similar to the reasons our ancestors came. Even people who escape penniless from hunger or terror bring with them something of value. They, like the pioneers of old, have determination and courage to overcome hardships. They bring knowledge, creativity, ideas and industry which will reinforce or improve the fiber of a free nation. They, too, must overcome poverty, hostility and language barriers, making adjustments to a foreign society that offers hope for a new way of life. With them, these new immigrants bring their memories and customs which, when comfortably adapted to a new society, will enrich the variety of America. These new neighbors will build new lives and share our future. Their children and our children together will be America.

We must meet our new neighbors with wisdom and compassion, seeking to learn even as we teach and sharing our common human experience for our mutual benefit. Although the task may not be easy or glamorous, it will certainly be worthwhile.

The Rev. Theodore M. Hesburgh
President, University of Notre Dame

THE NEW COLOSSUS

Not like the brazen giant of Greek fame,
With conquering limbs astride from land to land;
Here at our sea-washed, sunset gates shall stand
A mighty woman with a torch, whose flame
Is the imprisoned lightning, and her name
Mother of Exiles. From her beacon-hand
Glows world-wide welcome; her mild eyes command
The air-bridged harbor that twin cities frame.
"Keep, ancient lands, your storied pomp!" cries she
With silent lips. "Give me your tired, your poor,
Your huddled masses yearning to breathe free,
The wretched refuse of your teeming shore.
Send these, the homeless, tempest-tossed to me:
I lift my lamp beside the golden door!"

Emma Lazarus

Author and photographer Tom Bentz with Samoan children.

Introduction

"Fellow immigrants!" began President Franklin Delano Roosevelt in an address to the Daughters of the American Revolution, dressed in the finery of U.S. success. Offspring of tempestuous times—of tea-tossers who indeed rocked a pompous English king with their rebellion—these ladies had become, in but a few generations' rocks of the cradle of liberty, the rock-hard guardians of this new nation's own brand of storied pomp. In the isolationist roar of the 1920s and the following decade of depression, the golden lady of the New York harbor—the new colossus—saw the door nearly close to new immigrants.

Today, as then, we face the danger of forgetting who and where we have been. Ours is a fellowship of stomach-rocking sailboats, hellish slaveholds, and hip-to-hip packed steamships. Our forbears all came this way as immigrants.

Fellow immigrants, I invite you to come with me through the open doors into the lives of our newest immigrants—to follow the paths that have led them here and lead them on, to show what they bring, to see what they find here, to share what they feel. This is their story.

It is also ours. My grandfather came here at the end of the

last century through the then open door, one of the more than five million Germans who moved to America in the 19th century. He grew in the bilingual Wisconsin dairyland and came to prefer pumping beer to milking cows. He ran his tavern and his mouth at the same time. Once he ran a prohibited brewery in his cellar and landed in jail. He enjoyed all the privileges of a U.S. citizen without ever becoming one. He even exercised his inalienable right to vote.

Although he did father my mother, Herman Radloff was not a great American. His grave does get flowers on Memorial Day, but his story will only bring smiles over beer and bologna within my family circle. Still, he makes me a second-generation American, and a grateful heir to the country who let him in. Under the current national quotas and preference for persons of needed professions and proven skills, Herman never would have made it in, and I wouldn't be here.

I am the beneficiary of an immigration open door, the front door. Significantly, the Statue of Liberty faces east, toward Europe. Fortunately, for me and my ancestors, her features are Caucasian. She has her back to the eastern hemisphere. A century ago, during the same decade that she and my grandfather arrived from Europe, the U.S. Congress passed the Chinese Exclusion Act that effectively slammed the back door on immigration from Asia.

Not until 1965 did this European preference fall. Immigration has since doubled, swelled recently by the arrival of refugees from the east, west and south. A few of these fled natural disasters. Most are driven by the international forces of war, political and economic oppression, and the promise—or hope—of a better life.

The old colossus, a bronze statue of the sun god Helios, straddled the harbor of Rhodes twenty-two centuries ago. The new colossus, the Statue of Liberty, our marble and copper monument to the American dream, must now step into her second century and our nation's third with a stride and beacon that spans not just one harbor but all the oceans and tides. She stands for invitation and vision, not conquest and resistance. Many fear that she will soon be crushed by the unchecked flood of new immigration—of uninvited refugees and illegal aliens.

We need not fear the foreign. The patriarch Jacob did not catch the vision of Israel, the nation he was meant to be, until he had wrestled through the night with a stranger.

This year our nation, as it usually does about once in a generation, will test, reassert or redefine our immigration policy. This spring the sixteen-member Select Commission on Immigration and Refugee Policy completed its two-year task and presented to the Congress its recommendations for our future approach to those who choose to make this country their new home.

This book is not an analysis of history and law, though they frame our view from the first chapter on. It is rather a look into the real lives of those who are now entering our country. They are black, brown, golden, white. They come from all directions, by day and night, and by all means. They swim rivers, sail seas, fly oceans, walk deserts. They are here at a price and with a purpose. We will hear each of their stories in their own words and see them where they live and work and play.

Some waited in years-long lines at our embassies in their old countries. Others took sudden chances, thought to be last chances, to flee their homelands. Some have been here a few years, others a few weeks. These are their portraits in passage, drawn in the frames of the past, the forms of the present, and the dimensions of the future.

"Remember," as Franklin Roosevelt reminded the Daughters of the American Revolution, "remember always, that all of us, and you and I especially, are descended from immigrants and revolutionists."

Thomas Bentz

Prologue:
A Nation in Motion

Once I thought to write a history
of the immigrants in America;
then I discovered that the immigrants
are American history.

Oscar Handlin

Huki mai ke kaula—pull the ropes!
Huki mai ka lau—pull the sheets!
Pa mai ka makani—the wind blows!
Popoho na pe'a—fill the sails!

The bronze-skinned crew chanted in rhythm as their sleek
koa-hewn canoe cut through the navy waves, passed under
the sun, and crossed the unknown border into the North
Pacific. The sun behind them danced on their paddles as they

stroked and sang their way toward a new land they would call Hawaii.

These people discovered America more than a thousand years ago, a thousand years before a small string of English colonies declared themselves independent states. Their names, islands of origin, and the story of their passage are now largely hidden in legend and folklore, but one thing is sure, they were immigrants.

Our 200-year-old nation has a 20,000-year-old legacy of human immigration. Native Americans traversed Arctic icefields, open prairies, cascading mountains and russet deserts two hundred centuries before Europe was settled and civilized. Yet in just five centuries of sharing their two billion acres of land with the immigrants from Europe, these people who knew no boundaries except those drawn by nature are now confined to less than three percent of this country's least productive soil. It is a sad chapter in our nation's history that the first Americans, who were the most free and mobile, are now the most bound.

Their noble bearing through adversity is as worthy of emulation today as it was years ago when Thomas Jefferson paid them this backward compliment: "Shall we refuse the unhappy fugitives from distress that hospitality the savages of the wilderness extended to our forefathers arriving in this land? Shall oppressed humanity find no asylum on this globe?"

The poor treatment of native Americans can only be rivaled by the deplorable treatment accorded the group of involuntary immigrants that were brought from Africa in chains. They remained three-fifths human by order of the U.S. Constitution until the Civil War. The Civil Rights Act of 1965 finally declared their full equality under law. Black Americans remain among the poorest of this nation's citizens despite the rich contributions they have made to the building of this country.

The Laws of Naturalization

One of the grievances presented to King George of England in our Declaration of Independence concerned people's inalienable right to migrate: "He has endeavored to prevent the population of these states, for that purpose obstructing the laws of Naturalization of Foreigners, refusing to pass others to encourage their immigration hither."

Even then, the tides of reality had washed the laws away. James Wilson rose at the Constitutional Convention of 1787 to speak in favor of open immigration. He noted that almost all the general officers of the Pennsylvania line in the U.S. Revolutionary Army were foreigners. He also reminded his fellow delegates that three of Pennsylvania's deputies to the convention were not colonial born, including himself.

Although the British came first, the Germans were close behind. Although New England discouraged them, most of the colonies welcomed these Germans, and some colonists like William Penn, actively recruited them. He founded Germantown, Pennsylvania, in 1683. By 1747, three out of every five residents in Pennsylvania were German, driven here by war, poverty and the promise of prosperity.

The next major group of immigrants were the Irish. Though many had come the generation before, in 1820 Ireland replaced England as chief source of U.S. citizens. That year, the potato famine in their homeland drove 750,000 Irish to our shores. Suddenly the reception for immigrants started to sour. Employment fliers appeared that read, "No Irish Need Apply." In 1845 the Native American (Know-Nothing) Party was formed to oppose the immigration of Catholics. It also desired a long probationary period for all aliens before naturalization. Before it faded within a decade, it had elected seven governors, including the original states of Connecticut, Massachusetts, New Hampshire, Pennsylvania and Rhode Island.

On the national scale, however, only the infamous and short-lived Alien Act of 1798 interrupted the free flow on immigration in our nation's first one hundred years. The Federalist Act, authorizing the President to deport any alien he thought was dangerous to the government, was allowed to expire after the election of Jefferson in 1800. The following century saw more than four million Irish and eight million Germans land on our shores. In the middle of the century, Czechs, Scandinavians and Russians also appeared in heavy numbers.

By the time the Poles and Italians arrived at the end of the 19th century, the nation had turned to industry and the new jobs centered in the cities. The former slaves of the South were also drawn to the working cities of the North, looking for opportunity. As cities like New York became more congested and more "foreign," reaction against immigration grew. As one Manhattan editor wrote, "The floodgates are open. The dam is washed away. The sewer is choked. The scum of immigration is viscerating upon our shores."

A few laws were passed to skim off this "scum." Convicts and prostitutes were the first to be legally barred by a Congressional ruling in 1875. Other undesirables were defined and excluded in 1882: "A lunatic, idiot, or any person unable to take care of himself or herself without becoming a public charge shall not be permitted to land." The list lengthened in 1891 (polygamists, paupers, those with loathsome or dangerous diseases), 1903 (epileptics, beggars, anarchists), 1907 (feebleminded, unaccompanied children, tuberculosis sufferers), 1917 (illiterates), 1918 (subversives), 1950 (anyone the Attorney General believes might be a danger to the U.S.), and 1962 (sexual deviants). The 1952 Immigration and Nationality Act brought all these grounds for exclusion or deportation together in a single code that remains in force.

Although arguments against immigration have been raised

in the Congress since 1797, only particular disqualifications were allowed to enter the law until 1921 and no group of people or nation was collectively barred, with one exception. After the devastating Taiping Rebellion rocked China in 1848, some 300,000 Chinese landed in the West. After three decades of letting them in to harvest our fields and build our railroads, the blatantly racist Chinese Exclusion Act of 1882 slammed the door on China. Then in 1917 an Asiatic Barred Zone stopped entry from a wide area of east Asia.

Discrimination based on national origin was locked into law in 1921 when Congress fixed each country's annual immigrant quota at three percent of that country's residents within the United States at the time of the 1910 census. Accordingly, there were no limits on immigration from Europe, but near total exclusion of Asians. The 1952 act continued the quotas but in 1965 it was amended to a limit of 20,000 from any nation.

Discrimination based on national origin has not only been faced by would-be immigrants to our land but, in one of our nation's most shameful actions, also by a group of our citizens. In 1941, amidst the hysteria following Pearl Harbor, 110,000 Japanese living on the West Coast—70,000 of whom were citizens of this country—were taken from their homes and jobs and confined for four years in "relocation centers" that were virtual concentration camps. Even after their release, hostility and violence followed them home.

Wars, both hot and cold, still affect immigration policy. We took in 400,000 refugees after World War II, the wars in Southeast Asia issued forth more than 350,000 new Americans, and the cold war has brought hundreds of thousands from Eastern Europe and Cuba. Such large numbers of dispossessed raise awesome difficulties, but their acceptance is certainly more humane than what this country did in 1939. In that year, Congress defeated a bill to rescue 20,000 refugee children from Nazi Germany on the grounds that their admission would exceed the German quota, even though American families were waiting to sponsor them.

Driven by what John F. Kennedy called "a trinity of forces —religion, politics and economics," 50 million people moved to America in the last four centuries. It has been the greatest migration in human history. As Alexis de Tocqueville said after visiting the United States in 1820, "On leaving the mother country, the emigrants had, in general, no notion of superiority over one another. The happy and powerful do not go into exile, and there are no surer guarantees of equality than poverty and misfortune." Yet the newly fortunate too quickly forget equality. It was an Irish immigrant in California who led the fight to shut the door to the Chinese at the end of the last century.

The Immigration and Naturalization Act of 1965 abolished the restrictive quotas based on race and nationality but kept in effect a system of preference categories for those we hold to be especially desirable, chiefly those with immediate family in the states, "members of the professions" or "those with exceptional abilities in the sciences or arts," and "skilled or unskilled labor for which a shortage of employable and willing persons exists in the United States."

After signing the current law in 1965, President Lyndon Johnson stood at the base of the Statue of Liberty and said, "The days of unlimited immigration are past, but those who do come will come because of what they are, and not because of the land from which they sprang."

The people of this country spring from earthier stock than professional quotas. What has made this country great is not a collection of acquired or required skills demanded of those who wish to come, it is the will these people possess to meet and move with the changing needs of our nation. Said our first President two centuries ago: "The bosom of America is open to receive not only the opulent and respectable stranger, but the oppressed of all nations." It has been our good fortune to find among the unfortunate immigrants who came through our open door the following national treasures:

Albert Einstein (German), Nobel Prize-winning
    physicist
Alexander Graham Bell (Scot), inventor of the
    telephone
Enrico Fermi (Italian), Nobel Prize-winning
    nuclear physicist
Father Edward Flanagan (Irish), founder of Boys Town
Hideyo Noguchi (Japanese), cure for smallpox and
    syphilis
Joseph Pulitzer (Hungarian), newspaper publisher
George Santayana (Spanish), philosopher
Sergei Rachmaninoff (Russian), pianist, composer
John Udden (Swede), opened Texas oil fields
Samuel Gompers (English), labor organizer
Andrew Carnegie (Scot), steel magnate
James Audubon (French, via Haiti), naturalist, painter

No law can anticipate such contributions, and therefore, no law should exclude, unnecessarily, such future contributors.

Millions More

Alongside the names of the immigrants who have become familiar to millions rest the quiet lives and contributions of the others who have forged in this land a powerful nation. Here is an accounting of those who came from 1820-1912:

Netherlands	190,954
Switzerland	244,364
France	487,504
Scandinavia	2,014,245

Russia	2,712,316
Italy	3,426,377
Austria	3,410,379
Germany	5,411,444
England	7,951,671
Others	3,661,000

These people contributed more than their numbers. As the U.S. Census Bureau reported in 1900, "Immigration contributed 30 million souls to our population and 40 billion dollars to our wealth." And William Howells, writing in *Harpers Weekly* in 1909, brought it down to flesh and blood: "Today, most of the hard, rough toil of the country is everywhere done by recent inhabitants from Europe." What Howells failed to mention is that much of this work was being done then, and still is now, by blacks and Asians. In the twentieth century these two groups at the bottom of the economic ladder have been joined by nearly 20 million Hispanic Americans.

The change in regional origin of our immigrants can be seen dramatically in these annual counts by the Immigration and Naturalization Service:

	Annual Averages			
Origin	1950-59	1960-69	1971	1976
Europe	132,564	112,336	91,509	73,035
Latin America	61,899	130,206	148,971	157,741
Asia	15,016	42,77	98,062	167,425

In the last decade, legal and illegal immigration combined matched the record influx of 8.8 million who came to our shores in the first decade of this century. In the next decade, as we approach a new century, we cannot let our vision be obstructed by this country's ambiguous and unworkable immigration policy. We must not lose sight of the real immigrants, the flesh and blood people, who will be giving form to our future. As Reubin Askew said, "We must stop talking about the American dream and start listening to the dreams of Americans."

Listen to a few dreams come true. Look at a few immigrants and their portraits in passage, from Port-au-Prince to Miami, from Saigon to Honolulu, full sail into the future.

New Immigrants:

Portraits in Passage

CHAPTER 1

Feliciano y Diaz:

Happy Days in Miami

Nada puede sustituir a la persistencia
Nothing can substitute for persistence

The sign on the wall of Jesus Enrique Serrano's small print shop in Miami is more than a personal opinion. It is a statement of faith and a matter of fact. Taken from President Calvin Coolidge, this bilingual bill of rights celebrates the self-discipline and determined enterprise that have drawn millions from their native lands to pursue happiness here in our country. Jesus Serrano came from Cuba two decades ago and has built a strong and secure life in a new land. Like his namesake from Nazareth, this Jesus crossed the sea to step out on another shore—to restore the lost and explore the new.

Last year more than 120,000 other Cuban immigrants came to our shores. Mirella, Ricardo and Lester Diaz were among the first to reach Florida. Mirella had waited more than

1

two decades to be reunited with her sister and brother-in-law, Miriam and Frank Feliciano. This is their story. It is also the story of countless other families who once were divided but are now made whole.

Last Night in Havana

"There was a knock on the door at 3:30 A.M.," recalled Ricardo Diaz. " Mirella had an ache in her stomach. Every knock on the door, especially at night, we'd think it was the police."

This time it was their release. There was a boat waiting for them and many more at Mariel. The political prisoner under Castro was free to go.

" We were out of our home in Havana in fifteen minutes," continued Ricardo as he sat shirtless and barefooted in the backyard of his in-laws' duplex in Miami. Eager, even anxious, to recall their ordeal, he sat on the edge of his chair, drawing deeply on a cigarette and digging his toes into the long grass.

" We had to leave right away. But before we could go the government came to make an inventory of everything we had. Furniture, food, car, even our rings were registered. Before we left they put a stamp on the front of the house: Ministry of the Interior, Estate Value.' We had to give them the key but we didn't have to tell them where we were going.

"First we went to my brother's house. Then at 10 A.M. we had to be at the immigration department to pick up our documents. From there we were bussed immediately to the deposit center at Mosquito Beach. We had to leave everything we had except the papers we held and the clothes we wore. They took the title to my car, my driver's license, my thirty-six dollars, our rings and even our picture of Lester." Ricardo snuffed out his cigarette. Lester circled on his tricycle, given to him at the Orange Bowl on his first day in this country. The four-year-old did not see the pain in his father's eyes.

"I have a negative for a picture of my neighbor's house. Windows are broken. Angry mobs surrounded the homes of people who were trying to leave. Effigies of defectors were hung and burned. They were cursed and called rats and other names that I cannot express. In one case I know the government had to send protection for a family under attack. Eggs and stones were thrown at you if you went to the Western Union office to send a telegram to the United States."

Three-day lines of would-be emigrants jammed the public telephones in Havana during the mayhem of that first week of May 1980. They were hoping to reach relatives in the states and join the swelling boatlift to Key West. This sudden exodus began three weeks before when more than 10,000 Cubans poured through the temporarily unguarded gates of the Peruvian Embassy in Havana. They packed the compound and appealed for political asylum.

Castro acted quickly. The Cuban president provided water, food, sanitary facilities, a polyclinic and Red Cross station, and milk for the children. The government also decided to "authorize all those who request permission to go home and spend the night there and return when they so desire, assuring them permission to travel abroad by way of the Peruvian Embassy as soon as they have the consent of the country that wants to receive them and gives them a visa."

Quoting the Convention on Diplomatic Asylum approved in 1954 at the Tenth Pan American Conference in Caracas, Venezuela, the Cuban government noted the limits that had been drawn: "Asylum can only be granted in urgent cases. Urgent cases are, among others, those in which an individual is persecuted by persons or multitudes who have escaped the control of the authorities or by the authorities themselves."

Such persecution could hardly be proven at the Peruvian

Embassy. There were too many people in too little space. Time was running out, and intimidation was rampant. More than a million Cubans took to the streets of Havana bearing signs that read: "Abajo la Gusanera—Down with the Worms," and shouting, "¡Que se vayan!—Let them go!"

Ricardo wanted to go. He could have easily claimed that he had been "persecuted by the authorities." But he was not among those seeking asylum at the Peruvian Embassy. He remembered all too well Castro's 1978 agreement to free any political prisoners who could find other countries willing to accept them. This had led to nothing more than a trickle from the island to the United States, and even that was comprised only of those who were still in prison. Free from prison since 1969, his chances of emigration under this provision, nevertheless, were non-existent. Instead he had acquired a visa from Spain and hoped this tact would provide escape for him and his family.

The Diazes had also applied for a visa from the United States, like 250,000 other Cubans, but had waited for more than a year without hearing a word. Suddenly they were caught in the changing tide of government policy. With the pressure building in Havana, Castro sought to defuse the situation by transferring the malcontents to Mariel, twenty-seven miles away. He opened the port to foreign boats and issued exit visas to all those who wanted to leave. By so doing he forced the issue upon the United States.

It began with a pair of lobster boats chugging one hundred miles from Florida's Key West to Mariel and returning with forty-eight refugees. Then a shrimp boat brought back two hundred. Within a week more than two thousand had arrived in Key West. By the first week in May more than four hundred boats bobbed in the harbor of Mariel, their captains holding lists of requested passengers whose fare had been paid in advance by relatives in the states. For many, Mariel was not only a chance, but their only chance, to leave. For Ricardo and Mirella there was also Spain.

"We were waiting for word to pick up our tickets to Spain when we heard people were leaving Cuba by boat," Mirella remembered. "All of us who had applied to leave the country in other ways got telegrams saying we could go."

On May 1, Castro addressed his people: "We are rigorously, strictly complying with our watchword that anyone who wants to go to another country that would accept them can do so and that the building of socialism, the work of revolution, is a task for free men and women."

Two days after Castro's speech, Ricardo made his way to the Swiss Embassy and its U.S. interests section. "I went to see if my U.S. visa was ready. By our number on the waiting list we should have already been processed." But he never made it inside. "There were seven hundred political prisoners waiting in line outside the embassy to see if their visas had been approved. Then came the plainclothes police, carrying sticks, bats and blades. Since the ten thousand took over the Peruvian compound, the sight of seven hundred crowding the Swiss Embassy must have excited the police into thinking that this bunch was also up to something. The police moved in and beat the people who were waiting. Some of the people picked up pieces of block to protect themselves.

"After the crowd dispersed, I wondered why the U.S. offered visas to more than three thousand people at the Peruvian Embassy in a spur-of-the-moment embarrassment, but not to those of us who had been waiting two or more years, those of us who had been jailed for joining the resistance against Castro. The Cuban government said that since the U.S. would not give visas to the political prisoners it is willing to release, then Cuba will allow them to leave without visas."

The next night, with no warning, the knock came on the door. After years of following all the designated avenues for exit and being denied at every turn, Ricardo and Mirella Diaz were finally on their way to the United States.

Mosquito Beach

The night lay cool, the mosquitos still, in Miami as Ricardo described his last day in Cuba. "The morning was hot by the time we were bussed from Havana to Mosquito Beach. They declared a special consideration for political prisoners. The government did not want to aggravate us, so we were kept apart and given shelter. Others had to stand in the hot sun for five hours. The police let loose their dogs. Lots of people were bit, cursed and hit by stones and tomatoes. The sun went down but everybody was closely watched. From the moment we left Havana, the police followed us everywhere, even to the bathroom.

"At 2:30 the next morning we were put on another bus for the half-hour ride to the dock at Mariel, where we waited in a warehouse. At four o'clock we packed onto the fifty-foot motorboat Rody with 118 other passengers and nine crew members. Cuban officials insisted that each boat had to take four other evacuees for each relative specifically requested by a U.S. citizen. The evacuees were hand picked by Castro's guards from among those who had taken refuge in the Peruvian Embassy, and had since moved to tents at Mariel, where they too waited for a boat to take them away."

Searchlights swept the harbor while soldiers with automatic rifles watched from the shore for anyone who might swim for a boat rather than wait to be called. Ricardo waited and remembered that it was through this same port that the Cuban missiles came eighteen years before. Then he was fighting in the mountains with the resistance movement against Castro. This time the harbor held a carnival air.

Crews lashed their crafts together and exchanged visits.
Passengers chattered in anticipation of the adventure ahead.

"After sunrise," Ricardo continued, "we were taken out
from the dock to a marine ship where we watched for an
hour. Then at noon the Rody's eighty-horsepower motor was
started and we set out to sea—130 people in a boat built to
carry no more than fifty. We had water, a little food and very
little room. We sat shoulder to shoulder beside each other on
the deck. We had thirty children who were walking, and
quite a few who were not. There were a lot of pregnant
women. The women had to cover themselves with blankets
when they wanted to go to the bathroom.

"Soon the sky rained down upon us and the sea rose up and
rolled us on seven-foot waves. Most of us got sick and
vomited. Night fell halfway between Mariel and the Florida
Keys. The four-cylinder motor labored on in our slow and
dangerous mission. We knew not where we were, nor could
we turn back. We watched the darkness for the coming
light. Then at midnight came the blinking welcome. At first
it was just a sprinkle of light dancing a line on the horizon.
Some of us started to cry as the star-spangled banner and
dock of the Key West Navy base came into sight."

Ricardo and the others on the Rody were thankful that
none of them knew the horror of those who capsized at sea,
of the ten who were trampled to death, just twenty-eight
miles from Cuba, before a Coast Guard cutter could reach
them, of the three who suffocated inside the packed cabin
cruiser named Sunshine.

A Tricycle and Two Bottles of Olives

"I really appreciated the welcome we got at Key West,"
Mirella said. "The National Guard provided a place to stay,

food and clothes, and so many attentions. There was even special attention given for the sick, a mobile hospital. In Cuba, I'd been a slave. I feel more at home on this strange soil. Americans opened their hearts. Everybody clasped our hands like real brothers and sisters. If the young people here would only know how hard it is in other places to be free, filled, clothed, to have everything in hand. How precious freedom is! I had nothing to eat but as soon as I landed here I felt a peace of mind, just to breathe free and speak free. I still can't believe it. I tried so many years.

"In 1959 I came here for my sister's wedding. Miriam was able to stay here with Frank because he was a Puerto Rican and a U.S. citizen. I had to go back after the wedding. But I had a mind to come back. Then after Castro's takeover, Cuba and the U.S. broke off relations.

"I applied in 1960 for entry into the United States, but Cuba would not let me leave because my brothers were of army age. I kept applying for fourteen years. Everytime they said no. Then in 1974 I married Ricardo. The next year Lester was born. In 1978 the government authorized people who were or had been in prison for political reasons to leave Cuba. In 1979 we got our passports and the okay to go. So we applied again to the U.S. for a visa to come here. This time they approved our application but first they took those who were still prisoners at the time. We had to wait our turn. A year later we were still waiting for U.S. visas. Then the harbor opened up at Mariel, and we had a chance to go. But I still can't believe I'm really free.

"It was all so fast. Midnight on Key West. A bus to Miami. One night at the Orange Bowl with six thousand other refugees. There we had breakfast and lunch. They gave us toothpaste, soap, medicine, towels and even a tricycle for Lester. Ricardo called my sister. I just knew I wouldn't be able to talk to her. I just couldn't take it."

Miriam felt the same way. "I almost had a heart attack. I think I jumped to the ceiling. I couldn't believe it. I cried. Frank had to give me a tranquilizer."

Another bus ride, a day and night at the Opa Locka processing center, and Mirella, Ricardo and Lester were released. They drove to their new home, Miriam and Frank's house in Miami's comfortable middle-class section called Westchester. There Mirella fulfilled her dream of feasting on American food. "The first thing I ate were Vienna sausages and olives. I ate two whole bottles of olives. I was in shock! I told Frank I wanted to eat a whole chicken. Offer me anything and I'll try it."

Moving Recuperation

Two days after his release, Ricardo, classified as a conditional immigrant with only sixty days temporary status in this country, had a driver's license. The same day he bought a truck. "I asked the owner of the place where I got the truck if he knew of any places that might have a job for a mechanic. The man said, 'I need somebody. How about tomorrow morning?' I started the next day, just a week after we arrived in America.

"I am so surprised to see a country like this. There is no problem if I like to work. In Cuba it is hard to find a good job if you have been a political prisoner. You are the first to be blamed and fired. Here there is so much more than what I expected. You can go into a store and buy lots of things in mechanics that I didn't even know existed. Soviet autos are copied from U.S. models of thirty years ago.

"The average Cuban salary is $100 a month. Here you start at more than $100 a week. There Russian shoes cost $90 and polo shirts $40. Rice is rationed at five pounds per person each month, and milk is available only for infants and senior citizens. Vegetables and cereals are delicacies. If you are willing and can afford to go to the bolsa negra (the black market) you must pay $14 for a chicken and $16.80 for a pound of coffme. Clinics are free, but you pay for them at the pharmacy."

For Ricardo, Castro's brand of revolution is just as untenable now as it was when he first went to fight it twenty years ago. "In 1960, I joined the Movimiento de Recuperacion Revolucionario and went to Escambray to fight for freedom from Castro. We had help from people in the country. We got money, guns and direction from Miami. Almost everyone of our group of forty is now in Miami. A lot of them fought in Brigade 2506 in Vietnam.

"After six months fighting in the mountains I got shot in the knee and went to Havana. The help kept coming from Miami, and we just kept fighting. Then in 1963, Cuban troops took over the place where we were fighting. They took us right away, men, women and children. We had to leave our homes and possessions. They took the men to jail-like farms that Hitler would have admired. There were nineteen strings of wire in the three-meter-high, ninety-six-meter-long fence with a machine gun in each corner. At the Sandino Centro de Concentracion, six thousand of us were packed two hundred to a cellblock. I taught others how to read. Now there are more than 100 of my former inmates, including police and doctors, living in Miami. I've seen people who have lost arms, tongues and eyes in Cuban prisons.

"When I got there they sat me down and said, 'Ricardo Diaz, you want to talk? Yes or no? Either way, it doesn't make any difference. We know all about you. You'll be here for thirty years.' They put me in a cell by myself with no communication for eighty-six days. They took my clothes and gave me an overall with no shirt. They never called my name but gave me a number, 1,045. They told me if I lost my number I would lose myself. My cell had a mat but no bed. There was no window except one little opening through which a little food was slipped twice a day. There was a three-inch tube through the ceiling for oxygen and one light bulb. At ten o'clock in the morning and ten o'clock at night they let me go to the bathroom and have a drink of water. I drank like a horse.

"I was never tried or even charged. I was only later told that you were treated according to your crime. I was never hit though others were beaten. I had much peace there. What could I do? I waited."

Three years later he was released. All the letter said was: "Retained for three years." One year later, in September 1967, he and five others boarded a fishing boat and tried to escape from Cuba. It only proved to be a way back to bondage. "They'd been waiting for us. When we started the boat the police stopped us and arrested us for trying to leave illegally. When we were transferred to Sandino again, the head man said to me, 'You'll never leave this place.' I believed him.

"One day, two years later, I was suddenly called over the loudspeaker to go to the warden's office. I was told, 'Sign this.' I thought it was my death warrant. Then they said, 'You're free.' "

Curiously his freedom was not the result of the goodness of his conduct or the completion of his sentence. Instead it came because a friend who had been released a few weeks before had spoken highly of him to the prison director. Even though he was released his problems were far from over. For political prisoners it was extremely difficult to find a job, and even more difficult to keep it.

"Communism is like a snake. It sneaks up on you. It looks ideal when you read it, but when you live it in your flesh everything reads backwards. Instead of uniting families and the people, it divides them. Instead of freeing you, it slowly pulls like a net until all the fish are caught, drawn out of the water, and find themselves suffocating."

According to Ricardo, perhaps a million more are still in this net trying to break free. He wants them to have the same chance that he has had by coming here. "I thank the U.S. government for the opportunity to live in this country. To have and do the best job I can, and to have peace of mind."

Like many other immigrants, the Diazes' entry into this country was eased by the presence of family members who had come before. Frank and Miriam Feliciano were well established by the time the Diazes came, but the memory of their first few years in the United States is still very much with them. Frank and Miriam were spared some of the pressures that the new arrivals had to endure. Still, their story is laced with other troubles, some of which are much more profound. In light of these, their triumph is all the more remarkable.

Miriam and Frank

Frank Feliciano has been a dreamer since childhood in Yabucoa. The lean boy used to lie on a sandy beach in his native Puerto Rico and imagine what his life would be like in other parts of the world. "I always dreamed of marrying a Cuban girl. My father traveled a lot and I heard a lot about the beauties of Cuban women." Miriam confessed to similar visions: "I was always dreaming of my principe azul, my blue prince." From her earliest years she saved pictures of France and the United States and made elaborate plans to see them one day.

There the meeting of their beginnings ends. Frank is twenty years older than his wife. She was just seven when he came to the United States in 1948. As a Puerto Rican, U.S. citizenship was his by birth, so he came here and started a new life with great enthusiasm. Miriam was not as fortunate. One day on her way to school in the small Cuban town of Manzanillo, she fell down. The next morning she woke up blind.

"My parents cried and everybody felt sorry for me. I told them 'Look, this is not the end of my life.' I asked to go away to a school for the blind that was eighteen hours by bus from our house. They wanted to let me ride for free. But I didn't want pity, and I always paid.

"As a little girl I learned everybody has to face something. Somebody has to be blind. Why not me? If not me, it would be somebody else. It is physical. It will pass in this life. This is better than to be spiritually dead. That is forever. Even when it is dark and cold, you can be sunshine for others. When I wake up still breathing, I thank God. I have peace because I believe and trust in God who sustains me and mercifully takes me by the hand to enjoy every minute of life and to know that everybody is beautiful.

"I had an advantage. I could read before I went blind, so I just had to learn to do it with braille. I found it wasn't a handicap but an opportunity to learn and do something new."

When her family moved to Havana, Miriam continued to grow beyond her blindness. At seventeen she graduated from high school and began to assert her independence in other ways. One night she was listening to an international radio station that sought to match people for marriage. It was called correo del amor, mail of love, and she decided to send in a letter. It was eventually read over the air: "I want someone who is twenty-five to forty years old. Someone who is responsible. All I want is a good man. I don't care from where or what race. Let God decide. I want you to know that I am totally blind. If you want to feel sorry for me, don't pick up a pen. But if anybody wants to really get to know me, please write."

Frank Feliciano was sitting in his car in Miami listening to the program. He had heard other letters before, but this one held something more. He immediately responded. His letter was one of seventeen that came to Miriam. She was delighted; her mother was not. "The first thing my mother did was slap my face. A decent family doesn't offer its daughters over the radio. Mirella read to me all the letters. I answered every one with a thank you."

Frank's letter seemed the most genuine: "Please answer, and we can be good friends."

Miriam continued, "Our feeling grew stronger day by day. Every day I would put a letter in the mail. It was like a diary. All we asked from each other was to be sincere and honest."

Over her mother's objections Frank came to Havana for a visit and convinced the family of his good intentions. One week later, Miriam, Mirella and Frank flew back to the United States for the wedding. Mirella was a witness, and after the ceremony returned to Havana. Though she was only in this country for a short time, she knew that she wanted to return. It ended up taking her twenty years.

Out of the Crib

Miriam and Frank enthusiastically began their new life together in West Palm Beach. In 1960 their first child, Janne, was born, and in 1961 their second, Elaine, arrived. Shortly after her birth the family moved to California. "I was fascinated with this country, the cooperation and the opportunity, it is the crib for everybody," Miriam reflected. "Frank had a good job in West Palm Beach, but we heard there was better money in California and we headed for Bakersfield. There Frankie was born, but little else happened. It was too hot. It was siesta time from noon to four for the children."

Two years later they moved to Philadelphia, but only stayed a short while before heading back toward the West Coast. When they got lost in Ohio they decided to try bus. "We stopped at the Holiday Inn. Frank, Frank Jr. and Elaine all had asthma attacks. Janne was only five but she could already read enough of the paper to look for a job for her daddy. She found a nursery looking for a planter. The next morning Frank went after the job. I stayed at the motel with the children and the little bit of bread and sausage we had left. We waited until nightfall when he came back, all sweaty, and pulled sixteen dollars out of his pocket. We knew we couldn't afford to stay at the motel, so the next day we gave up the $21 room and went with Frank. We parked under a tree for an all-day picnic.

"When Frank asked if anybody could help him find someplace to stay with his family, a man whose wife had just died took us into his home. All we had were our clothes and our blankets. He spread out mattresses and let us sleep on his floor. The next night we found a place to rent."

Through the kindness of that man and other members of the local Baptist church, the Felicianos were brought into the community and the family of faith. They found real security and stability in Columbus, and Miriam turned her attentions to the growing family. Their last child, Miriam, was born there and her mother talked about the early days there with fondness.

"I didn't let them eat by themselves until they were almost five. They always went to bed at the same time. During the day, I put a different little bell on each of them so I could follow their sound. I never ran after my children. I would just call them, and they would come. They knew when they did wrong. They would come and tell me and hold out their hands for a spanking. I would always tell them why they had to be spanked and that I loved them.

"I taught them their ABC's on the typewriter. They would have to show me the letters on the keys. Before they went to kindergarten they could all read in Spanish. Before they were five they could knit and crochet. Every night before bed they would prepare the clothes for school or church the next day. I would tell them which socks and dress or pants to bring me and them I'd pin them together."

When Miriam, the youngest Feliciano, went off to school, her mother started working. "I went to a training workshop and got a job assembling fuses for Western Electric. My first day I made twenty-one dollars on piece work. The foreman said, 'My God, Miriam, people who have been working here for years are only making seven dollars a day.'

"I kept working until I was making four hundred dollars a week. I took out what belongs to the church and saved the rest for when it would be needed. When they told me I was working so fast that I was taking away work that could be done by four other blind people who needed it, I quit and took three correspondence courses for vending. After six weeks of training, I got a snack shop at a Chevrolet car dealer. I was the only blind, Spanish-speaking vendor in Ohio. After two years we were able to buy a house."

Shortly after this, tragedy struck. Frank and Miriam were nearly killed in a car accident. Miriam was in a coma for two weeks. Both of them were in the hospital for three months. Frank was on crutches for the next year. But they were not defeated. When they recovered, they began selling Avon products, door to door.

In 1977 they packed up their Avon inventory and moved to Florida. The cold Columbus winters aggravated their injuries. "We came to Florida for our health and some warmth," said Frank. "We worked from 6 A.M. to 2 in the afternoon. Then from three to nine. We sold Avon, ice cream, soap, gum, potato chips, perfume, candy, baby dolls, and bananas. The first day here I got a lawn mower and found four places that let me cut for twenty dollars. So the next day I had eighty dollars."

Miriam, meanwhile, took a test to be a Florida vendor. Three months later they were in business. After struggling financially for the first year, they were finally able to sell their house in Columbus and buy a duplex in southwest Miami. They rented out the other half and waited until one of their children, or ideally the Diaz family, might move in.

Now each day Frank and Miriam leave their home with its attractive brick facade and surrounding cushion of trees and grass and drive through the heart of Miami. They pass through Little Havana, the first Cuban stronghold in this country, and continue on to Jackson Hospital. There they set up shop and all day long service a line of nurses and orderlies. All the items for sale sit in neat rows around Miriam. Before her there is a small plate for the money. She fingers the coins, files them and finds the appropriate change. She leaves the single dollars open and folds, double or quadruple, the larger bills. She moves gracefully through the confines of this booth, and Frank attends the wider circle around her, filling orders, stocking supplies and cleaning up.

"I am happy where I am," said Miriam. "I like working here. Today was slow but we usually clear about four hundred dollars a week. And when it is slow, I have a chance to crochet. They offered me a cafeteria, a bigger place, but I want to stay here.

"Now there is a man who is trying to take this place away from me. He is blind and has only one arm. He now works in the customs building but he wants to have my place, so he is claiming seniority over me. We will have to go to a hearing before the state's blind services people and let them decide. Whatever happens is for the best. If not here, then there is another place, and a reason I don't know. If this door is closed, there must be another door. We always thank God for whatever happens."

An Open Door

The Feliciano living room and kitchen are always open. Everyone is welcome.

"I'm a widow without a family; this is my family," said Margarita Freirre as she sat at the table eating. "They call me cucaracha—the cockroach!"

"That's because nothing can stop her," laughed Miriam as Margarita finished eating and went into the living room to join the Diazes. When she left, her seat was taken by someone else and the endless round of eating continued. Frank served the steaming chicken and rice and passed around cold bottles of beer. "This is my refugee chicken," grinned Miriam. "The chicken flew back to Cuba!"

It was nearly midnight when the door burst open with more company and the scream, "Here come the refugees!"

Miriam introduced Bernado Jimenez. "This is the son of the man who gave me my first job in Havana. He spent ten days in the Peruvian Embassy before he was able to come here. There were 216 on his boat, all coming from the group on the embassy grounds. There was no great danger in his twelve-hour passage. The trip cost him nothing. It was paid for by the Cuban community here in Miami."

Bernardo happily threw up his arms, "Very good! Very liberty!" His friend Raoul agreed and added, "If you are religious, if you talk about your belief in God, you cannot go to the university. There are spies in the churches and in the classrooms in Cuba." Such resentment is not uncommon in these refugees. But a more telling indictment of Cuban life was expressed by Maria Hernandez, a Cuban-American. "I went to Cuba in January last year for the first time since 1967,when I came to Florida with my parents. My grandparents house where I grew up hadn't changed since I left. I saw my old friends; they all had children. They touched my hair and couldn't believe it. They have no shampoo or deodorant. I bought candy for the kids. All of them wanted to come here. One fifteen-year-old said, 'Put me in your suitcase and take me with you.' "

The discussion continued and became more bitter. Angry reflections and invectives rose like the volume of their voices. It seemed that by speaking loudly they were all looking for some release from the tensions they had suffered. Leaving one's country behind for another, no matter what the reason, is such a frightening and final act. When all these voices had trailed off and the guests had gone home, there was still a little boy sleeping in a new bed, in a new country.

"For the first week he was here, Lester was afraid to go out," Miriam recalled. "Every time we took him out of the house he covered his head. I told him that Papa Dios provided for him on the sea. Now he wants to know why God was so good to him to bring him safely here."

Second Generation

For the immigrants to this country, their lives must always, necessarily, be split between two cultures and two identities. They must continually balance their old lives with the new expectations they have found here. This problem does not exist in such an intimate and immediate way for their children. The second generation is often much more accepting of American life. Their assimilation is more rapid and it can carry with it a certain alienation from parents and the older ways of doing things. Fortunately for the Felicianos, they have struck a tenable balance.

Janne, their oldest daughter, nearly twenty-one, is a certified sheet metal mechanic. She finished the two-year course in one year, and now wants to take up flying. She is studying aviation administration and management at the Baker Aviation School by night and still works every day. "I pay for my own school and car, give half to my mom, and still have saved seven hundred dollars," she accounted. She does profess some interest in going to Cuba to meet her grandparents but would never stay there.

Her younger sister Elaine, a student of health and medicine at Dade South College, agrees. "I like Miami—the people, the atmosphere, the adventure. I want to stay." She is still occasionally surprised to find her mother waiting up when she gets home late. Miriam reminds her that, "Nine o'clock for me coming home was late to my parents. A lady never went out with a man before they were married. She never went from arm to arm."

"That's still true in Puerto Rico," added Frank.

Miriam, the youngest child, confesses to no curiosity at all about Cuba. "I don't want to go there. I'm not Cuban. I am an American." She still loves her parents deeply and is happy to be at home with them. "It's not like mother to daughter, it's like friend to friend. My mother is my best friend. Everywhere my parents go, I go. I feel right whenever and wherever I go with them. When I go somewhere without them, I call to let them know where I am. When I am home they satisfy my needs and make me feel comfortable."

Frankie, their only son, is the most reluctant Latin in the household. He is home less than anyone else. When the living room fills with Cubans kibbutzing in Spanish, he is nowhere to be found. His manner and music are American and he is the only one of the family who does not worship in their Cuban congregation.

"He hates anything Cuban," said Janne.

"He won't speak Spanish," added his mother. "I ask him something in Spanish and he answers me in English."

When asked if he ever wanted to visit Cuba or Puerto Rico, he replied, "No way. I want to stay right here!"

Go Away?

The reaction of many Americans to the massive influx of Cuban refugees is ironic in light of the Felicianos' generosity. We are a nation of immigrants, yet many of those who themselves have passed the Statue of Liberty—what poet Emma Lazarus called The Mother of Exiles—now would shut the door on any more arrivals.

After 40,000 Cubans had landed here within the first few weeks of the boatlift, a Gallup poll, noting that 200,000 more may wish to come, asked the American public how many more they thought we should accept. Apparently the welcome was worn out. Only half wanted any more to come, less than 13 percent would welcome them all, and 40 percent wanted us to take no more. This was before another 80,000 arrived in the following two months. (See Appendix A)

Congressman Dan Mica of West Palm Beach was caught in the middle. Mayors and county commissioners in his Florida district demanded that he get federal help for this flood of immigrants. "Some of my people want me to go down to the beach with a shotgun and ward off these invaders," he told congressional colleague Dante Fascell of Miami. Fascell understood. The same kind of ugly calls were jamming his lines.

Such suggestions were not merely the province of anonymous callers. In a meeting between President Carter and the Florida congressional delegation, Representative Richard Kelly suggested the use of military force to repel any boats carrying refugees to our shores. Carter responded, "I am not inclined to sink boats with people in them."

The problem was, nobody knew what the President was inclined to do. First there was silence. Then apparently the policy was one of open hearts and open arms. Then it changed again. Nine days later, two hundred boats were seized and their captains threatened with fines before being released. Meanwhile, the human tide rolled in, and the local authorities and the communities they represented had to do the best they could without an immediate federal response. Finally the President said that the room in his heart for newcomers had its limits. His arms were "open to receive refugees in accordance with American law." But there was no accord among the lawmakers on Capitol Hill.

The Senate Judiciary Committee, headed by Edward Kennedy, held a hearing in the midst of the influx. It scolded the White House for not moving fast enough to grant full refugee status and benefits to the first 40,000 new Cuban arrivals and to the 20,000 to 30,000 Haitians who have come here in the last decade. Next door, the House Subcommittee on Immigration, Refugees and International Law came down instead for stopping the influx and enforcing the new refugee law. (See Appendix B)

The Administration vacillated in the middle. It granted the new entrants temporary parole visas instead of full refugee status, and let the localities pick up the initial resettlement costs. Apparently the Administration was afraid of triggering a tempest in Miami's huge Cuban community. Because of mass immigrations in the last decade, it had bulged to over 300,000 people. Washington simply looked the other way as the sea shuttle continued.

This indecision was unacceptable to Huber Matos and other Cuban-American leaders from Miami. In a meeting with Deputy Secretary of State Warren Christopher, they refused Christopher's request to help stop the exodus. They instead demanded that the U.S. send boats and planes to bring everyone who wanted to leave Cuba.

The two-month-old Refugee Law of 1980 had already been badly shipwrecked. It supposedly scratched the prior preference for persons fleeing from a communist country, such as Cuba, in favor of allotments based on humanitarian concern. The law set a ceiling of 50,000 a year for refugee admissions, 19,500 of which were alloted to Cuba. In a few weeks the exodus from Mariel ate up the entire world's allowance.

"When everybody decides to disobey the law," warned U.S. Refugee Coordinator Victor Palmieri, "there aren't enough police in a country to stop them."

There were many others who thought this unchecked immigration represented a total disregard for American law. The city of Hialeah had citizens and officials grasping for order. "Now I carry a gun," announced Mayor David Bennett. "We've had an 88 percent increase in crime since last spring. This is not acceptable. So we're going to war."

But the local crime wave could not be blamed so easily on the rush of Cuban arrivals. Before the latest surge of immigrants, Miami had already moved past Detroit to become the murder capital of America. After the first month of processing, only 492 of the new residents were detained because they appeared to have committed serious crimes in Cuba. Similarly, several thousand cases of venereal disease and an occasional case of tuberculosis or mental retardation were discovered, but the incidence of disease on the whole was much lower than that among the U.S. population. These new arrivals proved to be a healthier, more law-abiding lot than those already living here.

If they brought any weapons at all, they were their hands. It was a working-class group. The elite and professionals from old Cuba had come two decades before. These 1980 entrants were masons, carpenters, construction workers and electricians. More than two out of three were men, one out of five was black. Half had at least one relative here.

Opa Locka and Other Camps

Within a mile of the expressway that loops Miami, Opa Locka, an old air field, had been turned into a reunification area for Cuban families. It housed the lucky ones. They would spend only a single night in the cavernous World War II dirigible hangar because they had someone waiting and a place to stay in the Miami vicinity. Many others came much less prepared and were much less fortunate.

At Eglin Air Force Base in Florida, phone calls tied the lines day and night as private agencies worked to match the 10,000 refugees there with friends or relatives waiting outside the gate, or living far away. Many of the Cubans had never seen the relatives they hoped would free them. They arrived with ten-year-old addresses and telephone numbers without area codes. They came with names changed by marriage or lost in the maze of metropolitan phone books where there are so many of the same names. After weeks of delays, hundreds of the refugees took up stones and bricks, stormed the gates and scuffled with military police. Others scaled the fences in the middle of the night and disappeared.

Such outbursts were not confined to Florida. More than 300 other Cubans being held among 19,000 of their fellow refugees in Fort Chafee, Arkansas, had an unarmed, laughing romp through the gates and around the local town. Though there was no violence, Arkansas Governor Bill Clinton was not amused. "The situation has gotten utterly ridiculous. President Carter needs to make it plain to the refugees that if they are going to come here they are going to have to obey the law."

As the heat of summer chilled to fall at Fort McCoy in Wisconsin, the hope of freedom changed to a fear of freezing for many of the 5,000 who waited there. More than 10,000 had already been processed through McCoy, but the final thousands, the young, single, unskilled males who were unfamiliar with the language, had not found sponsors or a home. Stabbings, beatings, rapes, and attempted suicides fed their fears and tensions. Among the 5,000 were 266 juveniles caught in the red tape between Havana and Washington. The U.S. would not allow American families to adopt them without the consent of their parents. But their parents, still in Cuba, could not be reached. No states would pick up the cost for foster care or counseling, and though Washington promised to pay, it continued to delay. Meanwhile the most daring and desperate went over the fence at the rate of a dozen a day. Finally the remaining refugees from Fort McCoy and 8,000 from the other camps across the country were sent to Fort Chafee. There the winter would at least be warmer. Even with such insecurity, their problems paled in comparison with those of some other refugees.

From Freedom to Captivity

"We came to this famous country to be free," read the statement of the 260 Cuban inmates at the new federal prison in Talladega, Alabama. "When we arrived in Florida we were asked if we had ever been in prison and we answered truthfully. We are not in accord with the regime on the island. In Cuba now you either have to have great luck or be a communist if you have not been arrested. We do not understand how we can be in prison when we came here to be free."

"We have come here as refugees, not criminals," pleaded a forty-five-year-old man who had not been in jail since 1956, when he was confined for petty theft.

Under our present immigration law, a previous criminal record is ample cause to be denied residence in the United States. But whose laws and which crimes apply? If all convictions in all countries were grounds for exclusions, then the likes of Dietrich Bonhoeffer, who was imprisoned and killed in Nazi Germany for plotting against Hitler, would be denied. Clearly some standards have to be set.

The suffering of these particular Cubans again brings into focus the confusion of the U.S. immigration policy. It is not surprising that the Cubans at Talladega cannot understand why they are being held, nor for that matter why they are being held so splendidly. The Talladega campus, newest of our federal prisons, looks like a suburban college with low brick buildings, wide lawns and playing fields. "In Cuba," reflected one of the new inmates, "even those who have freedom do not eat so well."

On the one hand we quickly confined some of these refugees while on the other we still watched in awe as others made the death-defying trip from Mariel to Key West. We wanted to be useful, but at the same time we didn't want to be abused. We tried to be open, but hoped we wouldn't be overrun. Naively, we set restrictions, then practiced exceptions.

Unfortunately, the whole episode was so confused and mishandled that emotions necessarily filled the void left open by the absence of coherent policy. To better understand the effect these new Cuban immigrants will have on our country, we should look to the lives of those already here.

Cuban Ingenuity

Like Jesus Serrano's print shop, Cuban enterprises have made Miami a boom town of commerce and construction. Cranes continue to stack up office buildings, banks and housing complexes. Miami has already become the stock exchange for an extensive international shuttle of Latin American trade. Cubans run seventeen Dade County banks. On any given day the Miami airport is packed with Latin Americans taking home goods purchased in Miami's 10,000 Cuban businesses. These goods are either unavailable or unaffordable in their home countries. The result has brought prosperity to the whole community. Unemployment is only 5.2 percent compared to the 7.8 percent national average. Cuban Miami's 1980 Trade Fair of the Americas sold $68 million of U.S. goods to Latin American customers.

In spite of this, some of the established residents of Miami are extremely anxious about the prospect of more Cubans in their community. Though Hialeah is now a majority Spanish-speaking town, last spring the predominately white leadership voted down a proposal to make local schools bilingual. The city of Miami has become so Latin that a downtown Indian boutique is named Tienda Indu. One local white pastor said, "My people are beginning to feel that the Cubans have taken over the city. It's hard to go into some stores and be understood if you speak English. After all, this is an English-speaking country, but we make it more important to speak Spanish." One store, with a bitter tongue in cheek, posted a sign, "English spoken here."

However the problems that southern Florida is facing now are by no means exclusively racial or cultural. Last fall the Dade County schools were confronted with an enrollment bulge of 18,000 Cuban children, plus 435 Haitians and 1,127 other nationalities. In response, a group of county taxpayers filed a class action lawsuit to expel the refugee children already enrolled and to enjoin the school board from taking any new enrollees unless the federal government picked up the extra $20-million bill. "The taxpayers cannot afford to pick up the tab," said Thomas Tew, lawyer for the group.

Negative attitudes toward the refugees center around the high cost of resettlement and the fear of loss of jobs for U.S. citizens. The 20-year U.S. tab for settling Cuban exiles has topped $1.3 billion. Dade County Mayor Stephen Clark echoes the same concern: "It's costing these communities millions." Residents of other American cities that have large Cuban populations, such as Union City, New Jersey, are experiencing similar problems. Union City Mayor William Musto relates, "We have no housing and our schools are filled. We absorbed these people before when we had the tools to do it. We don't have the tools today."

The degree of welcome for these newest entrants is often viewed in the context of how much wealth people think is left to go around. A 1980 New York Times/CBS poll found that 48 percent of those whites who felt their families had improved financially during the preceeding year said that they believed the Cuban refugees would be welcome. Conversely, only 34 percent of those who found their economic condition had worsened expected a welcome for the new Cubans in their communities. This reaction is not merely the province of non-Cubans. Said an Ivy League graduate who had come from Cuban stock, "The major worry is that they will spoil the pie for everyone else."

Still, it seems too easily forgotten that the people who have come here from Cuba are the most prosperous of all Hispanics in this country. Their income is equal to the average American and their housing is better than average. They have already rebuilt the dying shells of dormant northern citys like Elizabeth, Hoboken, Union City, and Weehauken. And their community services have eased the strain of the latest rush of new settlers. Their contributions will keep the cost to local and federal government well below the $2,000 per person needed for the Vietnamese refugees. If they are as successful as they have been in the past, they will keep most of the new Cubans free of the need for major social services in the future.

It would also be good to remember that in a larger sense the whole influx of Cuban refugees is not entirely the fault of the present Cuban government. Certainly all is not well in Cuban economics today. Castro publicly has admitted that in Cuba —as in the U.S.—there is "sloughing off, laziness and low productivity." But as Cubans loyal to Castro rightly contend, our trade embargo and twenty-year compulsion to isolate or overthrow him has indeed hurt the country as a whole. It has contributed not only to the mass migrations we are seeing now but even to the terrorists who kill diplomats in this country or who plot new invasions of Cuba.

There are now at least 750,000 Cubans in the United States. We cannot afford to take in the million or more who would be happy to join those already here. We cannot afford to wage an endless backdoor war against communism. But we can afford to take the opportunity to accept a socialist government next door. We can even learn from each other's strengths. They can use some lessons in capitalist imagination and we could use a few in material restraint and social cooperation.

Both nations need to understand that our revolutions are far from complete, that our problems will not be solved by jailing or exchanging our disgruntled populations. Nor can we close the chasm between us if we allow, or encourage, would-be invaders to use our respective countries as bases of operation. The far better course was shown to us in 1978 when the Committee of 75, a coalition of Cuban business leaders, workers, housewives, students and clergy sparked conciliatory talks with Castro that led to the freedom of 15,000 political prisoners and opened travel to Cuba.

Ricardo Diaz remembers his years of fighting and talks earnestly about the militant marching going on in Miami. He is aware that the latest tide of refugees has been taken as a sign of popular rebellion and that a group of 140 Cuban organizations in the United States has again called for the invasion of Cuba. Yet even as he talks a far more profound concern is circling around him. Lester is happily riding his tricycle. He has apparently forgotten his fear of the marching and shouting in the streets of Havana that he left behind. He no longer holds his head when he hears steps outside. He is in the home of Feliciano-Diaz—"happy day." If he follows the example of his aunt who came before, each new day will bring a new opportunity to rejoice and extend his circle of movement and trust.

He grows in the faith of a family that now together sings the hymn:

No temeré la lucha	I will not fear the fight
Si Tú a mi lado estás,	If Thou art by my side,
Ni perderé el camino	Nor will I lose my way
Si Tu guiando vas.	If Thou art my guide.

CHAPTER 2

Gerard Jean-Juste:

Stranger in Miami

We thought by coming here
we would be in paradise,
having milk and honey;
but it's nothing like it.
It's only and simply
a daily battle for survival.

It is more than a song. "Étranger-Stranger" is the lament of
an expanding group of people without a country. This com-
position by Michael Voltaire and Kombit Revolusione, a Haitian refugee band, is a refrain of frustration. It tells of a vision
lost. These people have crossed the sea but found the promised land unyielding.

Strangers short of paradise, 20,000 Haitians are now held
in what they find is a purgatory called Miami. They are caught
in the morass of ambiguous immigration policies and in the
hot clash of racial hostilities. Still, they do not want to go back
to Haiti. They came here in broken, leaky boats that couldn't

make the 800-mile return journey. Furthermore, they fear the persecution, much more dreadful than they suffer now, if they were to go home. So they wait. They are hungry. They are harassed by immigration officials. Some have been here for eight years and others might have to wait another eight years while the asylum and deportation hearings drag on.

The difference between the treatment accorded the Cubans and the Haitians is striking. No one understands or articulates this frustration better than Gerard Jean-Juste. He is a Haitian immigrant priest who has devoted his life to helping these strangers. This is his story.

Missing Passenger

"The cup of coffee was shaking in my hand," remembered Gerard Jean-Juste. The year was 1971. The place was a transit shed at the Port-au-Prince airport. "A gunman outside yelled, 'One passenger is missing,' but I couldn't move. I was trembling inside." Father Gerry was returning home after a seven-year absence. He had gone to seminary in Canada and then worked in New York. He was shaking not only out of fear for himself but also out of frustration at finding that after so many years the horrible state of his people was unchanged.

"I had lost sight of the reality of Haiti. At first I was nervous, then furious. Can this country still be so poor? The poverty invaded me. I just couldn't stay," he confessed. The view from the plane was too painful. The oppressive secret police were still in full force. The celebrated death of brutal dictator Francois (Papa Doc) Duvalier had not brought in a reign of peace and prosperity. It had brought instead the regime of Jean-Claude (Baby Doc) Duvalier. Father Gerry took the next plane out of Haiti.

Justice and Liberty

A cup of coffee was cooling on the edge of a crowded desk. The year was 1980. The place was a storefront in Miami's Liberty City called the Haitian Refugee Center. On the back wall hung a sign in Creole: "Justis ak libete pou tout moun— Justice and liberty for all." Behind the desk Father Gerard jumped from English to Creole to Spanish, from the telephone to face-to-face conversation. This center is the heart of a community in hiding and he is the heart of this center. There are 15-20,000 black boat people who have risked death at sea to escape the hunger and fear imposed by the Duvaliers in this hemisphere's poorest nation. Father Gerry directs services to as many as 600 needy new arrivals each month, offering them food, clothing and counsel to those who come with nothing but what they wear.

These people come from a country where half the workforce is unemployed, where four out of five people are illiterate and where half the children are undernourished. The average annual income in Haiti is $100. These deprivations are at the root of the Haitians' poor treatment in this country. The U.S. Immigration and Naturalization Service insists that these people are not political refugees, but rather economic aspirants. Because the current law makes no provision for economic refugees, more than 1,000 Haitians have been deported since 1973 when their mass migration first began. In the last seven years less than 100 have been granted political refugee status. Such policies assume a clear line between desire for freedom and desire for food. The people at the Haitian Refugee Center know that no such clear line exists.

"We appreciate the emergency food and clothing donated by individuals and churches," says center administrator Bettye Wiggs. "But our top priorities are legal aid and advocacy." Ultimately, freedom from hunger, whether in the

United States or Haiti, can only come when governments make a real committment to justice. In this country these Haitians at least have a chance. In their homeland the opportunity seems nonexistent.

When Father Gerry speaks of his childhood in Haiti you can hear the bitterness from injustice remembered. But also, like anyone who speaks of a home left behind, you can hear the warmth and fondness that such memories bring.

Lashes at Lescayes

"I was born at Dupas, a place where two rivers meet in Cavaillon, Haiti," Father Gerry reflected. "I had a good time there, playing marbles, eating mangos, swimming in the river. My mother was illiterate. I was illegitimate. She kept me until I was three, then she sent me to school at Cavaillon. She would come see me if I was good. The next year I went to Lescayes, the capital of southwest Haiti. I was four. I've been on my own ever since. I boarded with two cousins who were teachers in Lescayes. I was lucky to go to a Christian Brothers school.

"My cousins had a whip. The rule of the house was that I had to be no lower than ninth in my class of fifty-six. If I fell below that I fell under the lash. If I finished tenth, I would get twenty lashes; if eleventh, twenty-two lashes; if twentieth, forty lashes. The whip was also waiting if I let another kid beat me up. I couldn't get in the house or have any food until I went out and beat him back. All the fights I was in I won, except with one guy who was too big for me—so I got my cousin to back me up.

"I was even whipped for going to church. But I went to church anyway, and I went alone. I loved going to church, especially during Lent. The Christian Brothers punched my card each day. I went every day for forty days and they gave me a reward. I loved to sing and pray. I prayed to God, and he helped me. It seems I walked through my life like I was holding an invisible hand. I always knew the Lord.

"When I was eleven they asked our class who wanted to be priests. I wanted to, but I knew there was no hope for me. I couldn't be a priest if my parents weren't married. So I prayed for my father to come home and marry my mother." He never came, so Gerry went to Port-au-Prince and public school.

"At first I was lost. Then I became head of a group teaching young kids about Jesus. At seventeen I finished public school and my Bachelor I. The French equivalent of two years of college, a Bachelor II, beckoned me, but I still wanted to be a priest. I told my father. He just said, 'You're not going to have a wife?' My cousins wanted me to be a physician. They didn't know I couldn't stand blood and suffering." Then with the coming of Pope John XXIII, the priesthood opened to him. No longer could anyone be denied the priesthood because of his parents.

"I made a deal with a priest. If I succeeded through Bachelor II in Haiti, he would help me out of the country. I finished in 1965 and left Haiti for St. Joseph's Seminary in Canada. In 1969 I was ordained a deacon in Trois Rivieres. Then my cousin Francois, the one who backed me up in fights in Haiti, backed me up again. He sent me money so that I could come to New York. The priest who had helped me in Haiti was at St. Theresa's Church in Brooklyn. There I worked in the community, taught Spanish and attended all sessions of worship. I became the church sexton and learned how to play the organ." Despite his aversion to blood and suffering, he went to the hospital as a chaplain.

"Most of the twenty-five Haitian brothers who went to seminary with me quit on the way to priesthood. I couldn't quit. I had suffered too much to become a priest to stop when I was so close. So, on June 27, 1971, the feast day of the patron saint of Haiti, Our Lady of Perpetual Health, I was ordained a priest at St. Theresa's Church. It was a special feast and festival that year for all Haitians, in America and at home. We celebrated the death of Papa Doc that spring. We joked about a hunchback who stood straight up when he was told that Papa Doc was dead, and asked, 'Who will replace him?' When he was told Baby Doc, he hunched right back down.

"We all dreamed of going home. That's when I thought I would be a priest in Haiti. I got a ticket for Port-au-Prince and a transit visa. As a backup (Francois would have been proud of me), I got a visa from the Dominican Republic and a ticket for Puerto Rico." It was on this trip that he found himself shaking over a cup of coffee in the Port-au-Prince airport. He was unprepared for the impact of a homeland more desperate than he could remember. He flew next door to the Dominican Republic, then on to Puerto Rico for a few weeks.

"Then I made up my mind that I had to go back to Haiti. When I arrived at Port-au-Prince that fall of 1971, no one was expecting me. I got a motorcycle, learned to ride it at the place I bought it, and rode off into the country. I stopped at churches along the way, identified myself and always found a place to stay. There is a fraternity among priests in Haiti, a readiness to take care of each other. You don't get that kind of welcome from American priests, especially if you are black. When I reached home, my mother was surprised to see me. She was still struggling to keep her children in school and she was very proud of me."

"On my way home, the bus I was riding on was stopped at a checkpoint at four o'clock in the morning. The guard demanded fifty cents from each passenger and two dollars from the driver. I was the first one in the front of the bus and I said, 'I'm not paying.' Then behind me everybody began to pick up the chant. 'Nou pap peye—We are not paying!' A second bus pulled up, a third and a fourth. Soon we were all chanting the same thing. The harried guard called the captain, who arrived in his pajamas and said everyone could go. When we got back to Lescayes we all had to identify ourselves. A few days later I was arrested. They didn't tell me why, and when they told me to 'Put your butt on that bench!' I forgot all the karate I had learned in New York." He was freed that day by a fellow priest and was told to report to his superior.

"I went to the bishop. I had previously protested when Duvalier had come to Lescayes and stayed at his house. Now he wanted to be sure my voice would be far away. So he sent me to the countryside where cars cannot even go. I went by boat, and I went without pay. I refused to swear an oath to President Duvalier, thereby denying myself the thirty-dollars-a-month salary from the state. I chose to live instead on my savings from New York.

"I complained to the powers in Port-au-Prince that so many children in my parish were dying of malnutrition. Nobody listened. Disease was also rampant. There was only one stream in our little village of Les Irois, cloistered in a cove on the western end of the island. Donkeys, pigs, chickens and children would all swim and drink in the same stream. Then I got an idea. There is a small stream at the top of the mountain above the village. If we had a pipe we could bring clean water down from the mountain and make a fountain from which all the people could drink.

"I went to Port-au-Prince to ask for help and to share my plan. When I told them I came from Les Irois, the government officials asked, 'Is that in Haiti?' When I told them my proposal, they told me I must be crazy. They said it wasn't their business to supply our water. They couldn't even take care of the problems in Port-au-Prince.

"So I went back to Les Irois. I carried the first bucket of

sand and everyone pitched in until we had built a dispensary. We had a Canadian nurse who gave shots to the children. But we soon ran out of medicine. We had nowhere to turn. It was hopeless. Finally I asked the bishop for permission to leave. He told me to see another. The diocesan line ran along Les Irois and neither bishop wanted to take responsibility for me."

When Father Gerry left Haiti, he went quietly. He gave $150 to a friend who passed it on to whomever needed to be bribed. He got out; his friend got ten days in jail. "Back in New York I went to work as religious coordinator and parish priest at St. Clement's Church in South Ozone Park. This is where my honeymoon with black Americans first began."

The Road Back to His People

"I left New York in 1973 because I wanted to study and understand the American system better. In Boston I could serve as a priest during the day and go to school at night. I said Mass for the elderly whites, blacks and Spanish and I studied the U.S. Constitution, law, government, education and civil rights. I was happy as I worked and read and waited for things to get better in Haiti. While I was there, the fighting over busing broke out. Unsuspecting Haitians were the first to be beaten. Many of them understood neither the language being spoken nor the bitterness behind it. The angry white vigilantes did not care which black victims they attacked. I was beaten, my car was broken into and my apartment was robbed during the rampage by blacks and whites." Estranged from his own country, alienated in Boston, Father Gerry was again ready to move.

"Northeastern University gave us a two-week Christmas vacation in 1977. I went to the airport in Boston and flipped a coin between New York and Miami. Miami won. I spent the first week here quietly. Then a Haitian priest asked me to say Christmas Mass right here in Notre Dame Academy. I preached that we should as Christians take up our responsibilities in all areas of life, including politics, and change the world for the better. I spoke in English, Creole and Spanish. The people responded. Many asked me to stay. The archbishop invited me to concelebrate the New Year's Day Mass. That day was the first time a Haitian drum, dance, and song were ever heard in the church. Sadly, the black priest for that parish was replaced by a white 'missionary' who had been in Haiti. The new priest forbade the drums and threatened to excommunicate the nun who had brought them into the service and who had been helping the new Haitian fugitives who were at a loss in language and legal understanding.

"They wanted me to stay in Miami, even the archbishop. But I told them I had to go back to Boston. I promised to return on the first day of my summer vacation. The day after school ended, I was in Miami.

"I had written to the bishop offering my help, but I never even got an answer. So I made a few phone calls and was allowed to stay at the Catholic seminary on the southwest side. I waited for two weeks but the bishop still told me nothing. So I went to the Haitian Refugee Center and offered my services. Supported by gifts from churches and individuals, the center has been struggling since it opened in 1974. We try to secure clothes and housing and to stave off the starvation, intimidation and deportation of those who have risked their lives to get here from Haiti.

"Finally the church refused my application for this ministry because I had moved without assignment. So from June 1978 through February 1979 I volunteered all my time for the center and lived off my savings. The nun who was helping the refugees got me a place to stay at her parents' house. Still, I want to serve the Haitian community through

the church. But only last year did the Catholic Church begin
to come up with any money and real support for the center
and our services. I would like to say Mass on the weekends
and keep up my work in the community during the week."

According to Father Gerry, part of the difficulties he has
with the church as a whole stem from his outspoken views on
racism. He has maintained that skin color has a great deal to
do with the reception his fellow Haitians have received in this
country as compared to the lighter-skinned Cubans. "I wrote
and spoke out about the racism I saw in the church. That
made the hierarchy mad and meant no money for the center."

He has also directed hard criticism toward the church for
its policies in Haiti. "I accuse the church in Haiti of prostitut-
ing itself by consecrating the marriage of Baby Doc. It was
his wife's second marriage. It was an offense to Christ and to
the country. While the people were starving or wasting in
prison, the President spent $5 million on his wedding—
$300,000 for food, $100,000 for her ring—covering the stench
with two planeloads of flowers from Miami. Then the Polish
priest who has come to our parish sent letters to the National
Council of Churches and the World Council of Churches, the
prime sponsors of our center, accusing me of undermining
the church.

"I don't mind. I don't need money. I have social security. I
have the community. I have a Lord who says, 'If anyone is
hungry, feed him.' Also find out why he is hungry and who is
failing to feed him. So I want to go to Geneva and raise the
Haitian issue with the World Council of Churches.

"We have had some successes. More than twenty Haitians
graduated from high school here last June. There is a Haitian
pride that denies you are suffering, hungry and poor. But the
suffering is still too much. Even Dade County officials have
stated that starvation, not malnutrition, is the primary problem for the thousands of Haitian refugees in South Florida.
Starving people cannot live on promises."

Black Caldron

The streets radiate heat in the northeast quarter of Miami called Liberty City. Charred remains of liquor stores and gas stations that once were the wishful means of escape for the ghetto-bound, stand like abandoned altars to those burned up dreams. These shells mark the riots of May 1980, when Miami blacks struck back after the acquittal of four white policemen who had beaten a black insurance executive, Arthur McDuffie, to death.

There were more coals in this fire than a single case of police brutality. There has been a city tradition of leniency for white offenders and harsh punishment for blacks. The black unemployment rate is near 10 percent while only 5 percent of the others in the city must go without jobs. And there were a host of other ills most directly summed up by Mayor Maurice Ferre, "There is no question that poverty, lack of jobs, rats, and people sleeping ten to an apartment, were the underlying reasons." Liberty City and Little Haiti, right next door, are where the Haitians live. It is here where they are trying to build a new life.

Mayor Ferre continued: "There is absolutely no doubt, documented and all, that the Fraternal Order of Police in Miami has been the bastion of a racist group. They are mostly southern whites and they don't like Jews, foreigners and blacks. I blew the whistle, and now they're after my scalp."

Whether or not the Puerto Rican mayor survives the next election, it is clear that the Haitians, who are both foreign and black, come with two strikes against them. As in the Boston disturbance, innocent Haitians were the first to be caught in the crossfire of the Liberty City riot. One of them did not survive. A white policeman shot Lafontane Ban-Aime in the head. He was a Haitian Pentecostal minister who had been trying to make peace during the riot. His wife and six children were left behind to make a life on their own.

Mayor Ferre insists that it's time to talk about racism. "My God, until we cross that first bridge, how can we expect to solve the problem before us? We must repent before we can be saved." Such racism always engenders profound resentment, and it is no different for the Haitians. Yet it is a cruel irony of this story that much of the resentment the Haitians feel is directed toward people with whom they have so much in common—the new Cuban refugees. To understand this, we need only look at Cuban Miami. It sits south of Liberty City, just on the other side of the expressway, but in so many other ways, it is light years removed. Its glaring white condominiums mock the rubble of the black community. It is all commerce and growth. As noted before, all of Latin America is rushing to invest in Cuban Miami. It is little wonder that when the blacks saw all this wealth rolling by on the expressway they began to boil. Many of the new Cubans entered Miami on the right side of the expressway. Almost all of the Haitians did not.

"The key lesson from the last generation is that we really didn't set about to build an economic base in the black community," noted Ray Goode, president of the Babcock Company, one of the area's largest home builders. He is now actively seeking black subcontractors to work on new building projects. But the lesson learned may be too late, the response too insignificant. With the influx of new refugees, the city population bulged to 1.7 million and the number of new jobs needed to 60,000. Under these circumstances, and with so much of the black community burned out from the riots, emergency aid was absolutely essential, but much too little came.

President Carter visited Liberty City after the May 1980 riots but left promising nothing. Two months later $90 million in aid was offered, including loans to rebuild businesses, economic development, job training, improved security in public housing, and funds for rapid transit and health care. Yet according to Senator Lawton Chiles, the aid package had already been planned and would have gone to Liberty City whether or not there had been a riot or the new influx of refugees. At the same time, Miami business leaders proposed to raise $291 million for development in the black community with a penny addition to the sales tax. The county school board also asked for $1.3 million for job training, but the legislature said no to both requests. Instead it offered only $8 million in loans and grants and tax credits for riot-damaged busineses, and an $850,000 summer youth program.

This is the context into which the Haitians have come. Whether one believes racism is the root of their poor reception or not, it is undeniable that their treatment has been deplorable. One cannot blame them for feeling some bitterness and resentment when they see how other refugees have been treated. Since 1975 more than 300,000 Indochinese refugees have been received into the U.S., making us by far the largest recipient in recent years. In 1978 more than 30,000 Russian Jews were taken in, and in a few months in 1980 125,000 Cubans floated to Key West. This raised the number of Cubans relocated here in the last two decades to nearly 800,000. During the last decade when all these others were receiving relatively open-armed receptions, the Haitians kept coming. More than 10,000 have been charged by the Immigration and Naturalization Service with illegal entry. And this is just in the Miami area. Estimates suggest that 75-200,000 other Haitians are in the rest of the country and the vast majority of them are similarly classified as illegal entrants. It is little comfort to them that less than one hundred of their people have been granted refugee status.

"Legally, most of these people do not qualify as political refugees," said Richard Gullage, deputy commissioner for the

INS in Florida. "They come from a country which is considered to be a friendly nation by our state department. This means that any claim of political persecution would have to be validated. Not many of them have been able to do this, so it is obvious that most are running away from the poverty in Haiti. Right now there are no provisions in our laws for economic refugees."

"A Friendly Nation"

This division between poverty and politics is not obvious in Haiti or anywhere else. In Haiti, hunger, illiteracy and poverty are perpetuated and ignored by a Duvalier legacy of intimidation and torture. Under Papa Doc, the dreaded secret police, the Tonton Macoutes, roamed the country, meting out terror, extortion and death at will. When Baby Doc took over in 1971, word spread of the disbanding of the Macoutes, raising the hope for human rights. Based on such promise, the U.S. raised its economic aid to Haiti. But the secret police soon returned. They used new names, the Poto Mitan (Central Pillar) and the VNS (Volunteers for National Security), but their methods were the same old story of terror. The Haitian Human Rights Office was suddenly put in the Foreign Ministry. "Liberalization" was denounced. And the moderate leaders of the first opposition parties in twenty-two years were arrested three months after their formation. Baby Doc's 1979 Press Law officially made it illegal to "offend the Chief of State or First Lady, make any attack against the integrity of the popular culture, (or) erode public confidence in the country's financial system." Prison sentences were prescribed, and many were sentenced. Obviously the line between poverty and political persecution was drawn extremely thin.

Under the previous policy that was heavily influenced by cold war fears (Immigration and Nationality Act of 1952, Migration and Refugee Assistance Act of 1962), a maximum of 17,400 refugees per year were allowed into the United States, providing they met the ideological and geographic criteria. They either had to be fleeing from a communist country or from the Middle East.

With the passage of the Refugee Act of 1980 (see Appendix B) the annual ceiling was raised to 50,000 and the ideological and geographic limitations were removed. From the 16 million refugees in the world (see Appendix C), we could now choose those of "special humanitarian concern to the United States." The new law defined a refugee as any person forced to leave home because of racial, religious, or political persecution, or anyone who had a "well-founded fear of persecution" should he or she return home.

Many who have fled from Haiti have told the U.S. District Court, Attorney General Benjamin Civiletti, the Select Commission on Immigration and Refugee Policy, the Congressional Black Caucus, and the Organization of American States Human Rights Commission about just such well-founded fears. Max Julien said that his brother was arrested when he returned to Haiti from Miami and was imprisoned for four months at Fort Dimanche. Jean Louis, a former Tonton Macoute, testified in a sworn affidavit that he had received "standing government orders that anyone and everyone deported back to Haiti was to be arrested and imprisoned. The rationale was that if you left Haiti you must be against the government. Many die in prison and the length of stay varies from weeks to years, if you survive."

A military clerk said he had seen official documents authorizing and then confirming the execution of an entire group of Haitians deported from the United States. Another witness testified that 14 percent of his fellow inmates at

Dimanche from 1974-1977 were deportees from the states. Furthermore, a former inmate at the prison said he had been held in a cell with twenty other Haitians, all of whom had returned from Miami, and all of whom were manacled and looked "thin as skeletons."

Patrick Lemoine lost seven years, 100 pounds and nearly his life in Dimanche and Cassernes Dessalines, watching eleven of the twelve men in his cell slowly die in the spit and excrement on bare, wet concrete. They were accused only of criticizing the Duvalier regime. "The miserable rags we were given to wear became so filthy that they were taken away, leaving us totally naked. It took me two months to knit a blanket from the thread inside my mat, then that too was taken away. We were given a cold, ten-second shower every two weeks, eighteen squares of toilet paper per month, and rice portions so small we could almost count the grains. With no medicines, we had to treat the wounds of the beaten and bleeding with urine. When I was released, I was too weak to walk, but my spirits were sky-high. I learned later that it was the U.S. Ambassador to the U.N., Andrew Young's visit to Haiti and his pressure on Duvalier that led to the release of us political prisoners in accord with the Carter human rights policy."

This was in 1977. In 1978, Amnesty International reported: "There are no legal safeguards against arrest by the security militia. Hundreds of political prisoners have not been accounted for, dead or alive. Haiti has one of the world's highest mortality rates among detainees." In 1979 Marie Lucien Pierre reported that her husband Bernier, a Haitian-born Canadian school teacher, disappeared at the airport in Port-au-Prince at the end of their visit in Haiti. Two days later at the Haitian Refugee Center in Miami she learned that he was in prison at Lescayes charged with "incitation a la revolte," or as a Canadian official who helped press for his release translated, "Badmouthing the regime."

Fear of persecution is not left behind when the Haitians leave Duvalier's island. It follows them to sea and lands with them in Florida. Several boats have been caught on Bahamian reefs, drowning the passengers. Voyagers on other crafts have died of disease, hunger or thirst. Some boats known to have left Haiti have never arrived at any port. Others are stopped by the U.S. Coast Guard.

One quiet morning, in the pre-dawn darkness, a Coast Guard searchlight surprised a boatload of black boat people within sight of the shore at West Palm Beach. Suddenly the two smugglers, who were ferrying the eighteen passengers from Freeport in the Bahamas to Florida at $550 a head, fired their shotguns. They hurled infants overboard and forced the desperate adults into the water after them. Eight of them drowned, including a mother and her five children. "The water damn cold, deep," recalled Martin Prosper. "The only thing I know, I swim. I pray, 'God, don't give me up.'" When Prosper and the nine others made it to shore, they were immediately arrested as illegal aliens. They were told by the INS that they could not stay in the U.S. and must return to Haiti. If they did not leave voluntarily and instead asked for political asylum, then they had to go to jail. Only if they could post a $1,000 bond, or find an American citizen who would assure their appearance at subsequent hearings, could they avoid imprisonment. They had neither. It is a tragedy that such treatment is not uncommon.

In the West Palm Beach city jail, Father Gerard found an eight-year-old Haitian girl alone in a cell, weeping for her father. "This was an INS tactic to press the father into signing a paper promising he would go home," said Ira Golobin, a volunteer counsel for the Haitians. "Two years ago, INS launched an accelerated campaign to throw the Haitian refugees out, scheduling one hundred deportation hearings a day, making due process and legal representation impossible, and ending with a form letter saying that no matter what the defendant said, the claim for asylum had been denied."

In 1978 the INS also refused to extend work permits they had granted some Haitians the year before. Without the permits, these people were denied the right to work. And without official refugee or resident status, they were denied social services. If not for the church, they would have been denied food, clothing, counsel and legal aid.

Backed by the National Council of Churches, a coalition of expert immigration lawyers went to court to stop the deportation hearings against these Haitians. Federal Judge Lawrence King in Miami ordered the INS to suspend these hearings until he heard testimony from eyewitnesses on the "character of the Duvalier regime." The churches also filed complaints with the Inter-American Human Rights Commission against both the Haitian and U.S. governments for violating the rights of Haitian citizens. The National Council of Churches, sixteen state councils of churches, civil rights and labor groups, the congressional Black Caucus and the mayor of Miami have all called for granting asylum to the Haitians in this country.

Entrants (Status Pending)

On May 2, 1980, Presidential Determination 80-18 allocated $10 million to aid Cubans and Haitians arriving in Florida. But none of this money made it to the Haitians. On May 14, President Carter stated that federal agencies were "to receive the Haitians in the same manner as others seeking asylum." Still, the Federal Emergency Management Agency spent $50-60 million to aid the entry of Cubans, but only $150,000 to process the Haitians. This bias was manifested in other ways as well. The INS form 1-94 received by a Cuban read, "Asylum Applicant" while the I-94 given a Haitian in

the same legal category read, "Exclusion Proceeding." The
Haitians also received form I-122 ordering a court appearance to show cause why he or she should not be deported.
Cubans who arrived in Key West were released to waiting
families within twenty-four hours, some within the first thirty
minutes, after arriving at their processing centers in Miami.
Haitians with family in the area have had to wait up to three
weeks to see a doctor for health clearance and up to four
weeks for release. Cubans at the Opa Locka processing center
benefited from a computer which speeded family reunions, a
children's nursery, and information on education and
employment opportunities. None of these services was made
available to the Haitians at any location.

Under the Refugee Law of 1980, any refugee entering the
country is assured uniform assistance for up to three years.
Yet some of the Haitians have been waiting up to eight years
for acceptance into this country. Meanwhile they have been
denied basic legal and civil rights. The 3,000 who were picked
up offshore were classed as "excludees" and the 7,000 who
presented themselves to the INS or who were discovered after
entering the country were classed as "deportees" and required
to seek political asylum on a case-by-case basis that quite pos-
sibly could have taken another eight years. In light of this
confusion, on June 20, 1980, President Carter granted parole
to the Haitian and Cuban entrants which allowed them to
stay in this country legally for six months while the Congress
had time to establish their future status.

On July 2, Judge Lawrence King ruled that the INS had
knowingly violated the constitutional, statutory, treaty and
administrative rights of thousands of Haitian refugees seeking asylum. He ordered the INS to take no further action
against the 4,000 plaintiff-immigrants in the class-action
lawsuit. He was impressed by the testimony from and about
those who were beaten, tortured, and left to die in Haitian

prisons including those who had been returned from the U.S. He also found the treatment of the Haitians by the INS to be "equally stark." He said the INS had shown prejudice against the first flight of black refugees here and had failed to grasp the relationship of Haitian politics and economics and the evidence that dramatic poverty there is a function of the political system. He found the INS design to deport Haitian nationals and no one else was discriminatory, the abuses of the Constitution and the INS regulations were systematic and pervasive, and finally he said, "It must stop."

"Prior to the most recent Cuban exodus, all the Cubans who sought political asylum in individual hearings were granted asylum routinely," he added. "None of the over 5,000 Haitians processed during the INS program at issue in this lawsuit were granted asylum. No greater disparity can be imagined."

In 1975-1976, the last year such data were maintained, 96 percent of asylum applicants fleeing repressive right-wing governments that are supported by U.S. tax dollars were denied refuge here. Meanwhile, 95 percent of those seeking asylum from communist nations were granted sanctuary.

The June 1980 Carter parole classified the refugees as "Cuban/Haitian Entrants (Status Pending)." As entrants they would be entitled to federal and state social services and benefits, provided they report to the INS for their new documents. However, legislation must be submitted to Congress to establish the Cubans and Haitians as full-fledged entrants. With their status pending, the Haitians waited for their official welcome, depending on private contributions to meet their immediate needs. The Dade County Community Action Committee, which is trying to resettle the Haitians, was promised $500,000 in State Department funds. The contract was signed June 1. By mid-August, no money had arrived and the agency, unable to meet costs for food, housing, transportation and salaries, refused to accept any more Haitian refugees from the INS until it could find homes for the 230 Haitians in the Metro Hotel in Miami Beach. At the Krome Avenue INS holding center, 950 Haitians waited to be processed and placed.

"The place was made for 200 people," complained Father Gerry. "There is not enough shelter, sanitation is sadly lacking, and the fire protection is inadequate. The new director of the State Department's Cuban-Haitian Task Force in Miami, James Gigante, promised $16.8 million for the health and educational services for refugees from Cuba and Haiti. But in the meantime I have asked federal officials to clarify the present and pending status of our entrants."

In this maze of immigration stall and bureaucratic shuffle, the Haitian Refugee Center continues to provide assistance to these new entrants who come at the rate of 500 each week. "I'm scared," confessed Father Gerry. "I don't know where we're going. We're getting food now. But I've discovered pockets of people starving to death in Little Haiti. In an election year, we get promises and payoffs from President Carter—what Mayor Ferre calls 'pablum'—but after the election, forget it."

Port of First Resort

The United States has a history of generous and orderly welcome for refugees from such places as Hungary, Cuba and Vietnam. Communism was the common enemy from which all these people fled. As they left Europe and Asia, they all stopped at a second country and waited for our welcome. Cubans were the first to come here directly, but even so, the freedom flights of the 1960s and 1970s were well spaced and evenly accommodated. Then 1980 changed all that. The new

Refugee Law eliminated ideology as the cornerstone of acceptability. Flight from communism was no longer the only effective prerequisite for U.S. residence. Theoretically, flight from the right is now just as valid. However, in practice, we have been just as slow to accept refugees from dictators who uphold our capitalistic principles as we have been to criticize their oppressive tactics. The plight of the Haitians clearly and painfully points out the discrepancy between what the United States says and what it does.

Though the Cubans face less chance of persecution at home, they were allowed 19,500 entries in 1980, and took 125,000. The Haitians, on the other hand, were held within the stingy allotment of 1,000 immigrants for all of Latin America in the same year. As mentioned before, they have also been faced with up to eight-year waits for asylum hearings to prove they were political refugees in fear of persecution. Both the allotment and the enforcement of the law last year made a mockery out of the special humanitarian concern that was to be the basis of our future refugee policy. It is neither humane nor fair to limit all the Americas south of us to 1,000 entrants while allowing 125 times that number from Cuba to come in during the same year. We seem willing to empty Castro's prisons while filling those of Duvalier. What turns out to be "special" to us is our "humanitarian concern" for people like us. Fear of persecution is still not as compelling to us when thinking about the Haitians as is our fear of communism.

We will not, indeed cannot, accept all economic refugees, all the hungry and homeless of the world. International cooperation, economic aid, and peacemaking are much more humane and affordable means to address the refugee tide than are mass resettlements. What we have here and now, however, is no distant plea of Palestinians or Ethiopians for their homelands or for a part of ours. We have instead the compelling actions of two of our closest neighbors. On the one hand we said, "Stay away, for now;" on the other hand, we left the back door open and in they came. We demanded pure political motivation from the Haitians but not from the Cubans, who talk as much about the lure of American goods as any lurid details of life under Castro. We turn our backs on Castro, who has at least been willing to talk, and impose a trade embargo. Then we turn around and welcome his defectors with open arms and millions of dollars. Next door, we throw money to Duvalier, who—according to officials administering aid in Haiti—diverts 20 to 40 percent of the government's income into his family accounts. Then we turn around and send back his desperate people who flee to us. This is not a "friendly nation," as the INS insists, but only a friendly dictator. We who cry at the high cost of Haitian aid in Miami ought to be railing against the higher cost of welfare for Baby Doc, his wedding cakes, his corrupt village chiefs and his murderous secret police.

U.S. refugee policy is directly related to foreign policy. We create economic refugees by choking trade with Castro and by fattening Baby Doc. Having dangled the carrot, we cannot simply pull it away when the refugees come and want to stay. We must either work to improve the economic relations with and within our neighboring countries, or be willing to receive the people who end up suffering the consequences of our foreign policy. Whatever we choose to do, it should be made clear that this is a national problem. Local governments cannot be left to bear the burden of resettlement and accommodation alone.

Miami struggled valiantly to meet the immediate human needs of their new Haitian residents. But as Dade County Manager Dewey Knight said, "While the national effort to determine the status of Haitians goes on, the local community must respond to their needs with grossly limited resources." Just how much Miami, or for that matter the federal government, can afford to pay is a difficult question, but it must be answered. Dade County spent nearly $1 million last year for health services to Haitians.

"Today the American people must ask what more is expected of them," said Edward Kennedy to the Senate Judiciary Committee hearing on the Caribbean refugee crisis. "We must know what the number of new refugees will be and what our government is doing to cope. We can and must expect our government to plan, to organize, and to involve other countries in these critical humanitarian issues." So the call for international planning and cooperation must go out. And yet at the same time we must recognize that it is just such a lack of planning and cooperation that caused the refugee problems in the first place. Many countries would rather export their problems than deal with them at home. We also must realize that the U.S. itself is presently caught in the economic squeeze of recession. Kennedy concluded his statement by addressing just this concern: "America's door to refugees will remain open only so long as we prove to the American people that by admitting refugees we are not displacing Americans from jobs or opportunities, and that our government is administering refugee programs efficiently and fairly."

Kennedy is right to be concerned about American jobs. This issue is much on the minds of Americans in both Miami and the country as a whole. But if one looks closely at the plight of the Haitian refugees, compassion is called for in light of the discrimination they endure in their quest for employment. If the door to opportunity was open for them, it was open only a crack. In November 1977 approximately 6,000 Haitian aliens in Florida were issued work authorizations by the INS. With this license to work, many Haitians took jobs that were unwanted by U.S. citizens. For minimum pay, many rode out into the early morning darkness to spend long days cutting sugar cane and picking fruit and vegetables. Then suddenly a majority of these authorizations were summarily revoked by the INS by means of a mass mailing. This allowed the individual Haitian no hearing and no procedural rights, leaving him or her unable to seek lawful employment in the states. The inequity was astounding. On the one hand, the Haitians were subjected to individual hearings on their appeals for political asylum; on the other hand, they were denied individual hearings when their right to work was revoked.

On January 18, 1979, Judge William Hoeveler of the U.S. District Court ordered an injunction against the INS and for the reissue of work permits to Haitians. He ruled that, "as a result of the revocation of the work authorizations, Haitian aliens in South Florida have suffered and will continue to suffer malnutrition, substandard and overcrowded housing, mental and physical illness and the breakdown of the family unit. In the opinion of experts from Dade County, the employment of Haitians will not have a negative impact on the employment opportunities for American citizens or permanent resident aliens." This conclusion was supported by City Manager M.R. Stirheim: "Allowing immigrants to work does not appear to displace residents in the employment market."

Ironically, if anyone is likely to suffer from the access of Haitians to American jobs, it will probably be our own black citizens. Such circumstances are far from new. In 1933 black activist W.E.B. Du Bois wrote, "We have seen wave after wave of poor and ignorant and unskilled come into America, climb over our bent and broken backs and achieve success, honor and wealth, and thumb their noses in our face. Look at the Irish, the Italians, the Russian and Polish Jews, Greeks and the people from the Balkans. I am not jealous of them. I do not even blame them in the environment of race hatred in which they unwittingly come. I simply say that America will not let us succeed."

Still, there is somehow a binding beauty in the black struggle. In Liberty City, the resident American blacks whose sons and daughters already suffer the city's greatest unemployment, whose dreams must be dug again out of the rubble of the roots, are now reaching out to these new people from Haiti. At the Church of the Open Door in the heart of Liberty City, pastor Harold Long and a group of volunteer tutors teach basic English to the newcomers as well as help them through the confusion of the new world around them.

Priest in Process

The phone rang at 6 A.M. Father Gerry stirred slowly in the quiet apartment he shares with his brother. He had been up late the night before, teaching a weekly class of new Haitians the basic rudiments of communication and survival in Miami. The phone call was from a community group in St. Petersburg. They wanted to know, for publicity in the local paper, what he planned to say to them the next day. After he carefully explained the issues to the caller, he got up and slipped into his cleric attire, a black shirt and a white collar tab, and went to work.

Two hours later he stood before a local TV camera in the cluttered Haitian Refugee Center. His eyes held a steady sincerity that made you feel he was telling you, face to face, the Haitian story of sorrow for the first time. Behind him on the wall hung a painting of a man who had lost his wife and five children in passage here. Before him, out of camera view, sat the morning's group of silent witnesses, the survivors who had nowhere else to turn. When the camera and its sixty seconds of human interest were taken away, Father Gerry remained behind to minister to the needs of those around him. Shortly, the phone rang to tell him of another crisis at Miramar, the old school building where Haitians wait for immigration processing. Hardly a day passes without a problem there, but the mobile priest leaves his other duties behind and immediately drives to the old school.

On this day, like most others, Father Gerry found the refugees waiting patiently, in large groups, for a place to stay and a chance to go to work. All their possessions were in hand-held plastic bags. A single ceiling fan cut the heat in the stuffy assembly room where thirty people waited for a call from the man at the desk. Gerry was greeted by an INS representative and Roger Biamby, a Haitian who lectures in political science at the local Barry College and volunteers to help the refugees in his spare time. They talked in English, Creole and French. Soon the problem was solved. It was a misunderstanding about the asylum application form. The pregnant applicant, tired but reassured, sat down in the front row of desks. Behind her a dozen other Haitians waited their turns.

As Father Gerry made his pastoral rounds he came upon one room of forty young males who were silent at his approach but burst into chatter when he came through the door. They had been told they would have to stay there without food. He left them to investigate the problem, then returned. He assured them they would have food and a place to stay and that he would be back the next day to check on them. Then the young men relaxed, nodded and smiled.

Later that day, Father Gerard drove into Little Haiti and stopped at a driveway that was occupied by an old Chevy. Three small children, clad only in underwear, ran out to greet him. On the other side of the house he was greeted by their parents and an older sister. Over a back fence, a neighbor chatted. Under the umbrella of a tall tree, the shade and day stretched into a cool evening. The children bounced on the lap of their spiritual father as he traded stories of Haiti with their parents. As he talked, both he and his calling seemed to be lighter. After years of struggle, some of his people were at last entrants, perhaps on their way to becoming permanent residents, of the United States.

Yet these triumphs are not without doubts. Father Gerry has struggled here for many years and can see the problems still ahead. Even he is still a stranger in this country, a black man with status pending. On his way home in a land of hamburgers and tacos, he stops at a Haitian neighborhood restaurant, settles down for some spicy fish, fried whole, and hums his national anthem:

Pou peyi nou ak pou zanset yo	For our country and for our ancestors
Vanse an san-m.	We must look in the same direction.
Nan can nou nan poin trayi fre-n.	We must not betray one another,
Te nou se pou-n, sel met li.	Our land is ours, not for foreigners.

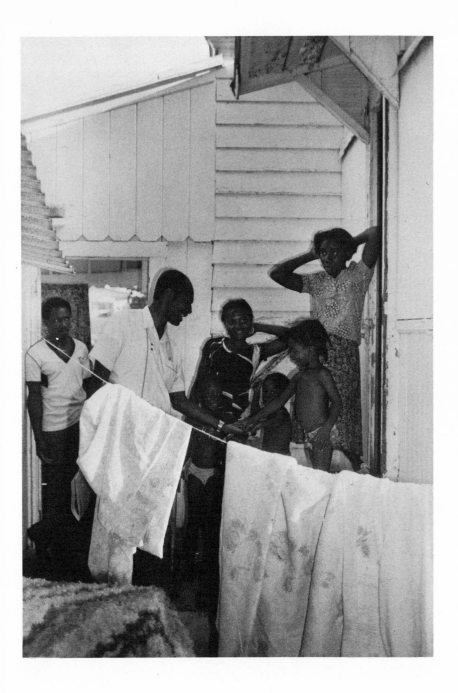

CHAPTER 3

Maria de la Luz Romero:

On the Border

Back in El Paso my life would be worthless;
Everything's gone in life, nothing is left;
It's been so long since I've seen the young maiden;
My love is stronger than my fear of death.

El Paso is the pass. It is the nexus of Mexico and Texas. It is an oasis from the desert below and the badlands above, a channel of opportunity and a net of apprehension. Here meet two cultures, two economies, two languages, two countries.

"El Paso," the twenty-year-old gunfighter ballad by country singer Marty Robbins, brought the story of two nations down to the lament of a cowboy who fell in love with a Mexican girl. America knows that Rose's Cantina now opens only in the balladeer's song and that the horses have long gone. Yet the image remains of a wild and wide open town of rugged Anglo wranglers and lovely Mexican senoritas, and there is still some truth in it. Inside that bar at the local Holiday Inn, the jukebox plays love songs for both countries while in the corner a

Texan in a cowboy hat holds the hand of a Mexican girl. But for most of the girls from Mexico, there is no one to hold their hands. Even those born in El Paso are much more likely to find their hands holding scrub brushes in someone else's home or pencils in the unemployment line.

Maria de la Luz Romero is a U.S. citizen. Her husband Jaime is not. She is in El Paso. He is in Mexico. They are separated by two obstacles. One is natural, the Rio Grande. The other is political, the U.S. immigration policy. This is their story. There are many others on the border who share it.

Wetbacks

"We had to walk miles through thorny bushes to get to the place where we had crossed the river before," began Maria de la Luz Romero. While carrying her four-year-old son, she followed her new husband through the desert next to Juarez. Being a U.S. citizen, she could have crossed into Texas over the bridge, but she had married a Mexican whose only way into the north country was through the water. "We stopped at the edge of the river, where the water was up to his neck, the current very strong. He found a wobbly log and, holding little Ramon on his shoulders, walked across the water. I told him to take me along. I wanted to cross the river with him. But the water swirled and the log trembled and I thought of the people who die trying to cross, someone nearly every week."

"I don't think I can get you across," said Jaime, looking at his wife on the other end of the log. So he stayed there and she came over the bridge the next morning.

Each year 82 million people cross the border legally, a quarter of a million a day. Three million a month cross the bridge at El Paso. No one knows how many people avoid the bridges and wade or swim the river, or pay smugglers to fly them over. One million are caught and deported each year for illegal entry. For each one caught, at least one—some say as many as ten—are able to make it into El Paso. Jaime Romero, like his father before him, is one who made it through.

His father worked here for many years, then went back to Torreon in Mexico to be with his wife. Jaime has been in El Paso since 1977. "I don't know what would happen if the U.S. put up the electric fence they've been talking about," Jaime wondered. "People are so desperate in Mexico that they'd find a way to come anyway."

The contrast just over the border is appalling. Ciudad Juarez sits with its open wounds like a beggar at the temple gate of El Paso. It is the third world face to face with the first world over a demilitarized zone of putrid water patrolled on both sides by border guards. About 25,000 paracaidistas, or parachutists, perch on the barren, arid hills at the fraying hem of Juarez, hauling the polluted water up from the river and huddling under whatever wood, tin or paper they can scrounge. They are not here for the lovely view of booming El Paso. Coming from a Mexican heartland that is suffocating under the burden of 50 percent of its people either underemployed or unemployed, they come for the barest hope of a job from their affluent Texan neighbors. Discarded cardboard boxes now disappear from the driveways of new ranch homes in El Paso and reappear as shelters for the desperate people on the other side of the border.

Nor is the contrast drawn only between the two cities. The line of distinction and denial also runs through downtown Juarez. It has become a center for international exchange and growth. Black and white Texas license plates roll the paved, well-lighted streets. They fill the parking lots, grabbing cut-rate gasoline, steak dinners for five dollars at favorites like Julio's Cafe Corona, and other bargains such as sun-ripened tomatoes for a nickel and coffee at two dollars a pound.

Across the bridge also roll the blue and white plates of the Juarez rich, who are seeking the better quality and snob appeal of U.S. goods.

Along with these people, there are about 50,000 authorized commuters who daily cross the 2,000-mile border. They live in Mexico but work in the United States. They are Mexican citizens with U.S. status whom David Simcox, U.S. State Department Office of Mexican Affairs chief, considers "permanent residents, even though they abandon this country every night." Meanwhile the homeless, jobless squatters along this tarnished border, and the millions more without jobs or hope south of the border, have only one means of entry. It is through the water.

Supermarket Stowaway

"I met Jaime at Rubio's supermarket in 1978," recalled Maria. "He was there twenty-four hours a day. He would open the store at eight in the morning, mark the merchandise, stock the shelves, mop and clean up until two or three in the morning. Then he slept there, guarding the place until it was time to open again. He was paid $35 a week. Later he was raised to $40, with $20 more for Christmas. He was afraid to leave the place, afraid he might get caught and deported.

"My son Ramon got lost in the supermarket one day. Jaime saw him, talked to him and brought him to me, still crying. So every time we went to the store, Ramon went looking for him, and Jaime would give him candy. Then one day he asked if he could come and spend the day with us. He started taking one day off a week, taking the half-hour bus ride to get to us by 3:30, then leaving so he could get back to Rubio's before closing at 9:30. I would cook for him, and we would stay inside. He was afraid to go out to a park. He still is.

"I was afraid to get serious. I had a rotten life. My parents were born in Mexico in Morelia Michoacan. I was born in El Paso where they opened up a bakery and stayed as permanent resident aliens. My older sisters, Aurora and Esperanza, were both born in Mexico and have to fill out a resident alien renewal card every year. My parents never went back, and I never felt like going to Mexico. My grade school was all in English. I started receiving bilingual education in high school. I had a good experience in the Anglo-Mexican mix. I felt like an American.

"In 1965 I finished high school. In 1966 my parents died. In 1967 I married Raoul Mata. In 1968 they took his passport away and revoked his visa when they caught him crossing the border with needle marks in his arm. But he got a false visa under another name. He had been on drugs since he was eleven and addicted since he was fifteen. He was nineteen when I met him. At first I didn't know he was an addict. Then I became too protective.

"He would come home and fall asleep. I saw the marks every day. He said he was giving blood at work. It got worse and worse. He couldn't keep a job. Then he got thrown in jail under a false name. His sister got him out on bail and he skipped bond to Las Vegas, where he wound up in jail again. He was in prison off and on from then on, for everything from traffic tickets to burglary.

"He only came home when he needed food. His family would get tired of him and kick him out and send him to me. I always took him in, then went to work at odd jobs, on and off, a wrapper in a department store, a moonlighting saleslady, or a dresser of models for a style show. They'd call me in the morning and tell me to come right over. I would work one or two hours a day, always at minimum wage. Finally I got a thirty-hour-a-week job in layaway at $1.60 an hour. All the time Raoul would come and go, never staying more than a week.

"We had five children I had to feed and raise. The three oldest, Ruben, Rachel and Raoul, live with my sister Esperanza now. She has bad arthritis and they help her and go to the store for her.

"I think I did wrong. I never told the children the truth about Raoul. I painted the picture of him too nicely. He would be nice to them and they would choose to go with him. But then he began to beat them. Once he even stopped the car on the railroad tracks with a train coming and the children screaming. In 1976 when Rosa was four and Ramon had just been born, Raoul and I separated. I applied for divorce in 1978. He said he would sign it but he didn't. Finally in September of 1979, when his sister threatened to turn him in to the police, he let the divorce be finished.

"The next month I married Jaime. Two months later Raoul died of an overdose of drugs. Always thinking he was just drunk, the children would undress him and put him to bed. They cried a lot when he died. He had just taken them out to a burger place. He was saving money to buy them Christmas presents, but they found him dead in his car with an empty wallet."

In contrast, Jaime was quiet and private. Though his wallet was far from full, it wasn't empty. Free of room and board expenses, because he lived and ate at the supermarket, he could use all his money for family expenses. His first child, Luz Maria, was soon born and she and the other five children depended on his support while Maria stayed home to raise the baby.

"In December 1979, Jaime got trained in the meat department," Maria remembered. He now had a skill. "Rubio didn't want his wife to know he was paying Jaime $60 so he gave him $50 from the cash register and another $10 on the side.

"When it started to get serious between Jaime and me, I told him that he couldn't support himself much less all of us unless he got his papers and became a U.S. resident. After marrying a U.S. citizen, a man has to establish a stable marriage, prove that he is the financially independent head of the household, and fulfill his Mexican military obligation before he will be accepted for residency in this country.

"Women have it easier. Under the old system, pregnant women could come through the river, give birth to their babies, and both mothers and babies would be U.S. citizens. Now only the baby becomes a citizen. Only when he or she becomes an adult can they sponsor the mother for citizenship. After the birth, the border patrol often evicts the mother, who then takes her baby along back to Mexico.

"I wanted to bring Jaime into this country as a legal immigrant under the top priority given to immediate relatives of U.S. citizens. But before he could be accepted here he had to prove that he had been working for six months at a stable job. Jaime went to ask for a letter on his employment at the market. Alonzo Rubio said yes he could have one, but he never got the letter. When Jaime asked why not, Rubio told him that he could only write one such letter every three years and this time he gave the letter to his own brother who wanted U.S. resident status."

At the end of 1979, Jaime left his makeshift home at Rubio's where he had worked responsibly for two years. He went to look for other work that could provide a way for him to stay with his wife and family.

Burden to the Bone

When Jaime came to this country he had not yet fulfilled his military obligation in Mexico. After careful thought and much discussion, he and Maria decided he should return to Torreon in Mexico and join the Army. When he was finished, he could get a legal passport and visa.

"He chose to go and finish his military obligation to Mexico," Maria explained. "But when he applied for service, he learned that he would have to wait six months before he could enter the Army. He would not complete service and get verification on his record until December 1981, and then his one-year limit on application for U.S. residency would have expired. We had done this because he had been told by the receptionist at the U.S. Catholic Conference Department of Immigration that he had to have the passport. That meant he had to go into the army. But when I called the American Consulate in Juarez, they told me he didn't need the certification and that I should call him right back.

"I sent him a telegram saying he should forget about the army and come back here. So he came back to me at the end of February. We went back to the Catholic Conference and got an employment letter from them that would allow Jaime to look for work in the U.S. while his bid for residency was being processed. We began to call or go see all the meat markets we could find, hoping for something based on Jaime's experience at Rubio's. Paramount was closing out. Peytons had just laid off 150 people. Four other places were also cutting back. Nobody was hiring. That was at the end of March. At the beginning of April we went to the El Paso Meat Company. The owner, Arvil Smith, asked if Jaime could bone. We told him yes, and he took Jaime into where the others were working and showed him the table he would be cutting on. Jaime was so happy."

"He was very polite," Arvil Smith recalled, "and sincere. I don't know what he can do. But I want to give him a chance. This is still America. There's still opportunity here. How can we close the doors to our Mexican neighbors and open our arms to all the Cubans?"

"Last year I found part-time work for six months with Mountain Bell," said Maria. "But at Christmastime I had to apply for food stamps for the first time. That caused more problems than it was worth. You see, when Mr. Smith signed the letter of intent to hire Jaime, we went right to the Catholic Conference. We asked to see the person we had spoken to before. They said we had to have an appointment to see her. We were given an appointment for two weeks later. When we came back with the letter in two weeks, we were told the letter was not acceptable because it did not say how much the company would pay Jaime. So we went right back to El Paso Meat and the woman in the office filled in our letter right away. It promised $3.10 an hour for forty hours a week, time and a half for overtime, and it pledged to hold the job open for Jaime for ninety days.

"Then we went right back to the Catholic Conference the same afternoon. Both of us were very happy and Jaime was proud of his letter. But when we got to the conference, thinking things were really opening up, the receptionist told him that he needed a Mexican passport, that he had to have been in the same job for six months, and that he was a burden on the state because his family was on food stamps. Jaime felt very bad and embarrassed when the woman told him he was a burden."

"They're right," Jaime reasoned. "I shouldn't be here. I should go back to Mexico. I told the woman I would work anywhere if I could be guaranteed that immigration wouldn't bother me. She said that they could not guarantee anything. You just have to find yourself a job. But my father worked here for years on the railroad in La Mesa, New Mexico, and he is now getting Social Security payments in Mexico, but he never got a pension. When everything is ready, something comes up to stop me."

With more than a trace of bitterness, Maria summed up their frustrations with the immigration process, using an increasingly popular analogy: "I have seen Mexicans who have waited in long lines at U.S. Immigration, just to be told that they could not be helped. Why then, is it so easy for the Cubans to come in?"

Family Reunification

"My God, I've got a place to help me!" Maria thought when she was referred to the Trinity Coalition. It is a church-sponsored, community-directed agency dedicated to the development of services to the newly arrived and needy in El Paso.

"Our number-one priority today is to get families together legally," said Luis Alfonso Velarde, Jr., speaking for both the U.S. Catholic Conference Department of Immigration and the Trinity Coalition. He directs the former organization and sits on the board of the latter. The coalition is an unapologetic advocate for the rights of aliens, a point of view that is very close to Al Velarde's heart. After sixteen years of dealing with immigrants in El Paso, he knows his job well. "We can pinpoint the eight states, even the villages, in Mexico from which most of these people come."

"We can't slam the border shut," interjected Minerva Antuna, the director of the coalition's Family Reunification Program. "The whole town would close down. Half of the local working females would not make it to work because their Mexican maids would not be able to come to their houses."

"People don't leave Mexico because they don't like the country," added Victor Azios, another Trinity Coalition board member. "Mexicans come here out of economic necessity. We need to develop more jobs and industry within Mexico. As Mexico industrializes within this decade we will see the influx of people slow down. We cannot tolerate open entry. We must deal with our limits openly and realistically.

Most important, we must cooperate. Mexico is proud. We must reestablish U.S.-Mexican relations on the basis of neighbors working together. With the joblessness in Mexico and the hopeless backlog in U.S. immigration processing, we are forcing desperate individuals to break the law in order to survive. And to break up their families in the process."

"There is only one Immigration and Naturalization Service examiner in El Paso," explained Al Velarde. "There is an eighteen-month wait just to take the citizenship test. There is a six-year wait for resident aliens seeking a visa for relatives. I think it's time to sit down with Mexico and be honest and say, 'We know with your rising population that you can't and won't come up with enough jobs for everybody. So we'll find a way to open and legalize the flow into the United States on one condition: you've got to let us help you with labor-intensive industrial development inside Mexico.' "

These three people have devoted much of their lives to helping aliens like Jaime to be united with their families in this country. They have a deep understanding of the problems in Mexican society that force aliens to seek a better life in the United States. They also understand the incredible difficulties that confront aliens when they try to enter this country legally and to find any kind of employment. Minerva Antuna explained one of the many catches in the system. "You can apply for welfare as a legal resident alien. But if you then apply for citizenship while you are on welfare, your application will be denied. So people try to get off welfare when they are ready to apply for citizenship. Once an application is complete, INS would consider food stamps as an example of dependency on the state. You cannot become a legal resident unless you work, and you cannot work, legally, unless you are a legal resident. The alien gets lassoed from both sides."

This is in large part the problem that faces Maria and Jaime. Minerva Antuna is trying to help them by getting

Maria employed so that the family can get off public assistance. "I've applied for jobs since before I had my baby, for more than a year. With what we have, it is impossible to make it. I get $222 a month from Supplemental Security Income for two children, but there is nothing for me. I am cut off because I'm married, regardless of whether or not my husband can find work.

"I went to the Texas Employment Commission every Monday for two months. One morning a grower called in and fifty people quickly lined up and were gone to pick in that field. Last time I was there I waited all day and no numbers were called, no announcements were made. At five they told us all to go home. I came back the next morning and waited until noon when I finally got a card for a regular appointment once a week. I got all my jobs on my own. None through the employment commission. They give you no leads, no help. You must go looking, then prove to them where you have been each week.

"I never felt anger," Maria said calmly. "I feel lucky to be an American. My oldest daughter Rachel is on the honor roll in school. I used to get punished for speaking Spanish in school, but Rachel can use both Spanish and English. She's a regular private eye, she wants to know everything. I am very thankful that my children have the opportunity of learning and growing up here. I am happy too that there are people like Minerva and the Trinity Coalition to help people who have no way to do it on their own."

Maria's sense of optimism is supported by Al Velarde's projections of future policy. "The new quota system proposed by the Select Committee on Immigration will reemphasize the reunification of the immediate family, spouses, parents and children, and it will deemphasize the extended family of brothers and sisters. But we must remember to treat Mexico and Canada differently than the rest of the world. The 20,000 annual quota for Mexico is ridiculous. It must certainly be raised to 50,000. We are neighbors. We trade freely and we must now move freely. Our families and our economies have long extended across our divisions. We must see that no border patrol is ever going to stop a family from being one if they have that vision."

To stress the need for rapid change, Velarde explained that the immigration problems in and around El Paso are getting more complicated all the time. "In my sixteen years of working here all of the immigrants have been Mexican, but in the last six months we've gotten the first El Salvadorans—we're handling twenty-seven of their cases right now—Guatemalans, Peruvians, Argentinians and Chileans. We even had two Nigerians who were just sent out of El Paso. They were caught trying to come in, claiming to be U.S. citizens. They were incarcerated in a camp for five months and then got out on a $500 bond. They applied for political asylum on the basis of tribal persecution. They were members of the Ibo tribe that fell from power and then were forced off their land. They were willing to work anywhere, doing anything. But they couldn't work without Social Security cards, and they couldn't get the cards without a work authorization. I couldn't get anyone to give them the authorizations. I sent them to a boarding house with empty rooms, but when the superintendent saw they were black, there was suddenly no room. All of Africa was allotted 1,500 refugee admissions to the U.S. in 1980, although two million fled Ethiopia alone last year.

"In the early wave of European immigration, the ethnic organizations like the Polish Immigration League were the real forces for the empowerment of the newcomers. Religious support came only from Catholics, Lutherans and Jews in those days. Today, other denominations have teamed with them to make religion the biggest lobby in Washington on behalf of the new immigrants.

"I'm Catholic but now I'm on the board of the Protestant-based Trinity Coalition. It is a real catalyst that is getting a lot of people in El Paso working together on immigration issues. I've seen too many government programs that are bullshit from the top to the bottom, with nothing good getting through to the people. Now is the time for people of faith to sit down and say, 'Let's forget our labels and remember that we have one task. To help these people who are following our footsteps or who are forging their own. We have a chance as one religious vehicle to speak and act, to change not only negative attitudes to the newcomer and border-crosser, but also the circumstances which set those attitudes.'"

"We can't do it all," concluded Manuel de la Rosa, director of the Trinity Coalition. "Yet we can and must, as people of faith, open our doors and work together to serve the poor, the alien, the lost, the seeking whom the system has failed to meet and accommodate. We cannot just open the border to all, nor can we secure it with a great wall of fence. We will find our security only in service to the most forsaken, in shaking the foundations of unfair systems and resetting them in justice, being most generous to those who need us most. We cannot just take the people from Mexico who face financial desperation. We must make relations between our nations more like a family, working together so its members in Mexico need not run away from home."

Balance and Respect

If we are to arrive at a more reasonable immigration policy, our relations with Mexico must change. The intimidation and duplicity with which the U.S. has always treated Mexico must stop. Some steps in a new direction were made in 1976 when Jose Lopez Portillo was elected President of Mexico and became the first chief of state to visit the Carter White House.

This visit was filled with pomp and circumstance and many hoped that it heralded a new age in the relations between the two countries. But such symbolism should have been accompanied with substantive changes in policy if it was to mean anything at all. Unfortunately it wasn't.

Within the same year, President Carter announced a new immigration plan that infuriated our neighbor to the south. Mexicans did not challenge his decision to act against undocumented aliens by bolstering the border patrol and fining employers who hired undocumented workers. But they were rightly offended that he did not even consult Mexico before announcing a plan that was certain to cause major economic and social changes within Mexico. The plan included a proposal to legalize the status of Mexican immigrants who had come to the United States before 1970, but it left in limbo the millions who had arrived during the last decade.

Furthermore, at the end of 1977, the U.S. scratched a proposal, already signed by six distribution companies in this country, for the purchase of Mexican natural gas. This left Portillo hanging by his fingertips. When Washington tried to resume negotiations the following fall for the same natural gas, the proud reply was that none was available for sale. Portillo complained that Mexico got "neither priority nor respect" from the giant to the north. In 1979 when Carter visited Mexico City, thousands of students and workers took to the streets to protest his presence.

Nevertheless the balance has since tipped toward reconciliation and respect. One need look no further than the monstrous oil find in the southern states of Mexico to find the cause. In just five years Mexico has turned from an importer of oil to the world's sixth largest exporter. Mexico now produces more than two million barrels a day, about twice the amount coming through the Alaskan pipeline. Tapping and controlling the flow of this oil is not the answer to all of

Mexico's problems, but it certainly is a start. Now our neighbors must look to controlling their ever-expanding population. Presently it is increasing at more than three percent a year, which means that the number of Mexicans will nearly double to 120 million by the turn of the century.

"Our oil revenues permit better financing for development," asserted Lopez Portillo. "The solution to our migratory and demographic problems lies in strengthening our economy. We must export products, not people."

The U.S. and Mexico now do $9 billion in annual trade. Mexicans think that if the U.S. lowered its trade barriers and made a concerted effort to stop illegal contraband from crossing the border, this figure would be much higher and in the process dramatically aid Mexico's plan to rebuild its economy. Yet most estimates maintain that it will take reduced sizes in Mexican families as well as rises in trade to enhance the economy. It will take ten to fifteen years for the fruits of Mexican oil and gas production to reduce emigration significantly. Border control depends on birth control. Meanwhile, more than half a million Mexicans will enter this country illegally every year. Most don't want to stay. They merely want to make enough money to sustain their families in Mexico and then return home. Tariff, quota, diplomacy and national debt are not in their vocabulary. Theirs is a simpler call: to survive.

At the beginning of this century, four out of five Mexicans lived in the countryside, one out of five in the cities. By the end of this century, four out of five Mexicans will live in the cities. Already this basically agricultural country cannot feed itself. Last year it imported more than $240 million worth of meat, beans and cereals. With rich natural resources and huge tracts of fertile uncultivated land, there is more than a little hope that Mexico can improve itself. But what the people of both the U.S. and Mexico must understand is that Mexico is now throwing away its most important asset, its people. The exploitation of Mexican workers by both the U.S. and Mexican profiteers must stop. If we can accomplish this, the best interests of both nations will be served.

New Mexico

Finally, in all our dealings with our southern neighbor, we must not forget that our own Southwest was taken from Mexico within the last 150 years. Spanish people were established there before the Pilgrims landed in the East. Not until Mexico was driven back in 1848 did the land now known as Arizona, New Mexico, Nevada, Utah, California, and Colorado became part of the United States. New Mexico is old Mexico. The Spanish influence there is not the result of a sudden intrusion of illegal aliens. Spanish culture flourished there while so much of the rest of the country was still waiting for settlement and civilization. Before the Mexican-American War, all the people in California were Mexicans. Turning our backs on Mexico and its problems is like turning our backs on a large part of our own history.

Latin influence runs through the blood of people on both sides of the border, as it runs through Maria and Jaime. Part of this life blood is the durable Catholic faith that inspires their lives, teaching both passivity and passion, soft resignation and strong resolve. Maria told of a journey they plan to make: "Jaime made an oath to take his first check when he gets a job, buy candles and flowers, and take them to the mountains of Christo Rey to the shrine of Santo Niño, the shrine of the child Jesus. I told him, 'You tell Jesus that I want to tag along with you.'"

CHAPTER 4

Jim Lockwood:

Border Patrol

Paso rio, paso fuentes;
Siempre te encuentro lavando:
Los colores de tu cara
El agua los va llevando.

I pass a river, I pass fountains;
I always find you washing there:
The water reflects
The colors of your face.

This folk song from Spain belongs as much along the Rio Grande as along the Manzanares. The man who sees these sights as he passes along the river in El Paso speaks Spanish but he is not Spanish. He is not brown like the river and the faces it reflects. He is white. And the people he finds near the water there are not washing but waiting for him to pass so they can swim the river and find a place in El Paso to hide. Still, the melancholy tone of his song is appropriate to these surroundings.

He is Jim Lockwood. He works for the U.S. Immigration and Naturalization Service Border Patrol. His job is to try to stop the people on the other side of the river from coming into this country and finding illegal employment. It is impossible and he knows it. He is not an immigrant, but he has compassion for those who come, criticism for those who exploit them, and a refreshing sense of humor about the hopelessness of the situation. This is his profile on behalf of those who cannot be shown or named.

Rio Grande

The river reflects the passage of time and people. By day its color turns bronze like the slick bodies that splash through this shoulder-high ribbon of water that separates Mexico from Texas. By evening, the color changes to a drab, brown reminder of the soil washed away from upstream banks. During the night it covers the traces of those who spend the day playing on the other shore and those who crossed it to come here. To Juarez, the Rio is both a sewer and a reservoir, a cesspool and a swimming hole. It is a means of refreshment and a means of escape. To El Paso, it is a source of water and a source of cheap laborers called wetbacks. There are three million legal entries into El Paso from Juarez each month but no one knows how many illegal entries. More than three hundred a day are apprehended.

"We probably catch about one in ten," guessed Jim Lockwood, as he stood beside his car marked Border Patrol. A few feet away stood the ten-foot-high fence that runs along the Rio Grande through El Paso. Its forbidding top curls toward Mexico like a menacing claw. There is an opening in the fence large enough to drive a tank through. The futility of his job couldn't have been more obvious. The Border Patrol has only 2,000 officers to watch the entire 2,000 mile border.

With just 300 patrols on line at any one time, its presence is less than the police force of Houston.

"Juarez cops beat and shoot people crossing the river. When they make it here and we send them back, they are often met by gangs who rape them and beat them," Lockwood complained. "I've seen limbs and lives lost by those who were running or hiding in this rail yard. And on the other side of the tracks is the city canal where some fall and drown. Last Saturday night a five-year-old girl dropped into the canal and drowned. She had been left with her brothers, ages eight and three. We found their parents in a bar.

"The bars are full of prostitutes who pour over into El Paso on the weekends. When we brought one of the girls into our detention center, she thought she was still going to turn her trade and work her way out. When we approached her to read her the charges, she raised her dress, showing no clothes underneath."

Jim got into his car and resumed patrol. In the distance he saw a small boy in shabby clothes walking quickly along the railing of a highway overpass. He pulled over next to him and called out to the boy and then got out and bent down, speaking to him softly in Spanish.

"What is your name?"

"Ramon."

"How old are you?"

"Nine."

"Where do you come from?"

"Juarez."

"What are you doing here?"

The boy shrugged, holding his eyes down.

According to Lockwood he was probably on his way to probe the refuse in El Paso's alleys and driveways, looking for something useful. Or he might have been going to empty the repeatedly pilfered Salvation Army boxes. Lockwood put him in the back seat and drove to the detention center. At the single desk in the receiving room that seemed too big for such a minor crime and little criminal, Ramon was read his rights, and he signed his X on the form that said he would return to the other side of the border. Inside the two large cells along the walls, dozens of other majados—apprehended aliens— waited for the trip back to the border. A few were children, some were frail old men, but most were young men. They were all silent, apparently resigned to the deportation cycle.

Ramon went back across the river and Jim returned to his patrol. Almost immediately he saw another young man walking slowly along the road. He turned at the approach of the patrol car but kept on walking casually. Aliens often run or try to hide at the sight of the border patrol, but even though this young man looked at ease on this side of the border, Jim knew from experience that the boy should be checked out. We pulled up beside him, Jim asked the familiar questions and was surprised to learn that the young man had come all the way from central Mexico. Even after being cap- tured at the end of so long a journey, just one block over the border, there was no anger or resistance. There was only resignation in his eyes as he climbed into the car for the ride to detention and deportation.

The INS estimates that three million aliens try to sneak into the U.S. every year. One million of them were caught in 1979 but many fewer in 1980. This decrease was not the result of fewer people trying to enter, but rather the strain on INS per- sonnel caused by the registering of thousands of Iranian students and the resettlement of more than 100,000 Cubans. The Border Patrol is hampered as well by the rising cost of fuel that has forced a 65 percent cutback in gasoline con- sumption. "We were left with only two cars patrolling the border here," Jim complained. During the summer of 1980, El Paso, the world's second busiest port of entry, lost fifty of its

350 Border Patrol officers to Florida for the massive Cuban resettlement.

Mexicans and More

The people who cross the Rio Grande are persistent and resourceful. Some come repeatedly, and are caught repeatedly, even though their third apprehension leads them to jail. Even though the situation is tragic there are times when the schemes are so foolish one can't help but laugh. Still, they come: some on foot, some by kayak or skateboard. "One guy without legs comes across with a skateboard," Jim Lockwood related. "He pulls himself through a hole in the fence, drops down onto his board and then gets picked up by a guy with a bicycle. It's incredible to see him latched onto the back of the bike, being pulled along on his board at breakneck speed."

Though Mexicans comprise the majority of illegal immigrants coming across the border (approximately three out of five), they are not the only ones. Others come from troubled Central American countries like El Salvador, Honduras, Guatemala and Nicaragua. They even come from as far away as Europe and Asia.

"At the bus station," Lockwood reported, "we've picked up Swiss, Germans and South Africans with expired tourist visas. Then another time at the border, four men from Belize tried to use the great American pastime, baseball, to win them passage to the U.S. They walked across the border wearing baseball caps and high-topped tennis shoes. But they not only wore sneakers; they walked like sneakers. It was a giveaway. We spotted them right away. No self-respecting American shuffles along with his head bowed. Americans would have been bouncing along with their heads bobbing."

Sometimes it takes only one word to foil a fugitive's entry. "A guy from Nigeria came across the border in a bonafide American business suit. But then he opened up his mouth and said, 'I am from Ah-lah-bah-mah.' " This chorus of international intrigue began to sound like a borderline rendition of "The Twelve Days of Christmas" when Lockwood added: "Today we picked up four Polish gypsies."

"We check every exiting vehicle," he said. In the process they find some delinquent local dignitaries as well as the illegal aliens. "We picked up a local official on the bridge checkpoint trying to slip through with his eight-month-pregnant Mexican mistress. We also stopped a local priest with a young male Mexican passenger who jumped out of the car and tried to run away. We found that the priest had used four young aliens for sex. He was quietly removed by the church."

Such sexual favors also present a problem in some of the more comfortable homes in El Paso. "We get calls from local Anglo women asking us to come and get their Mexican maids when they find that their husbands are cashing in on some sex on the side. They're happy to use the wetback women at starvation wages, as long as their husbands don't use them too.

"Every Monday morning, hundreds of women from Juarez come to the river, hike up their dresses, hold their shoes and wade toward work on the other side. We can pick up 400 waiting for buses to take them to their employers' homes. Some have one-day passes but most stay Monday through Friday for $40 a week. This is exploitation. If we pick them up, their employers complain and tell us how their great generosity makes it better for these women than if they had to face the hopeless poverty in Juarez. I tell them that if they really care about the welfare of their maids, they ought to pay them a minimal, living wage.

"We don't pick up anyone while they are working. Employers used to call the Border Patrol on Friday afternoon and tell us to come get the aliens, so they could send them home after a week's work without having to pay them a penny. Now we will come to take them back to the border only after they have been paid.

"We found one guy who was keeping three wetbacks in his warehouse, sleeping on mats and getting $30 a week. When we got there he wouldn't let us in. He told us to get off his property and assaulted one of the officers while the three aliens ran away."

Not all the aliens stay in El Paso. Some head much farther north. If they can't walk or don't know the way, some pay fees to smugglers, "coyotes," to take them where they want to go. "I was on vacation up in Evansville, Indiana, at a rest-stop restaurant," Jim recalled, "when I saw the door to the kitchen open. A young brown man balancing a basket of dishes came through. I knew as soon as I saw him that he was wet. I called him over and we talked in Spanish. He was lonely and hungry and had paid a coyote $500 to get him to Chicago."

Others don't get as far. Last summer, thirteen aliens from El Salvador baked to death in the Arizona desert where they had been abandoned by smugglers who had brought them across the border from Mexico. They died in the 150-degree sand, huddled against a scrawny bush in a desperate search for shade. Three of the women had been raped by a smuggler before he died. They had each paid $1,200 for the passage to Los Angeles.

Thirteen others in this group survived by drinking their own urine. A Border Patrolman who interviewed the survivors found that they had been well dressed and totally unprepared for the desert. They were toting suitcases filled with books and winter clothing. When he asked whether they had fled persecution from the right or the left, they replied, "Both."

This disaster is not unique in southern Arizona. A few years ago eight aliens were found dead in the same desert.

And the year before that a truck plunged into a flooded creek and killed all twelve aliens trapped aboard. Many other aliens die in less spectacular circumstances. "Disease is rampant," said Jim Lockwood. "They come across with tuberculosis and syphilis. A wetback with typhoid fever was working in a restaurant. We even found one case of the plague."

Meanwhile, in Mexico, the public health budget has been cut to the bone to enlarge the share for education. The funds left are insufficient to train and employ enough health professionals to serve what has become the world's fastest growing population. In the face of this disease and despair runs the dirty Rio Grande. As diplomats from both countries try to solve the problems they share, the people who cannot wait, the idle and hungry, will continue to cross the river. And just as surely, some of them will be caught and sent back by men like Jim Lockwood who understand the limits of the law that bends and breaks on both sides of the border. He patrols the middle where the desperados make their breaks, and the river reflects their faces.

CHAPTER 5

Joe Razo:

Sweatshop Sleuth

Mexico mi patria
donde naci mexicano
dame la bendicion
de tu poderosa mano.
Voy a los Estados Unidos
para ganarme la vida.
Adios, mi tierra querida,
te llevo en mi corazon.
No me condenen
por dejar asi mi tierra;

la culpa es de la pobreza
y de la necesidad.

Mexico, my country
where I was born a Mexican,
give me the blessing
of your powerful hand.
I go to the United States
to make my living.
Farewell, my beloved land,
I take you in my heart.
Don't condemn me
for leaving my land in this
    way;
the fault lies with poverty
and with necessity.

"Adios del Inmigrante–Farewell of a Migrant" is a contemporary Mexican folk song, or corrido, by Ettore Pierri. It is a bittersweet anthem of the Americas that starts far away in Mexico but can be heard clearly and passionately in many of our own neighborhoods. It is the song of los invisibles–the invisible ones–who stoop to pick our grapes, make our beds, wash our cars and dishes, and sew our clothes in small garages and shops that weave in and out of so many of our American cities.

These people come out of necessity, fleeing the poverty of Latin America and Asia. They are wanted only for their sweat. Like ghosts of the Great Society, they are afraid to be found, to speak up, to fight for their rights. But there are people who fight for them. One of the allies for the aliens is Joe Razo. This is his story, and it is theirs.

Concentrated Enforcement

Broadway in downtown Los Angeles is the midway of Mexamerica, a mix of cultures and commerce, The Orpheum Theater where Al Jolson once performed now plays Hollywood movies dubbed in Spanish. Blacks, whites, Asians, and Hispanics all walk the streets speaking in their native tongues and shopping in specialty stores that cater to every possible nationality. New sleek steel Japanese banks stand beside old brick and stone structures. Still, the street, in sight, sound and smell, is predominantly Spanish.

Spanish music spills from tocadisco shops. Taco, tamale, enchilada and burrito aromas waft from carts and counters along the way. The 81 percent white majority that ruled Los Angeles in 1950 is now a 44 percent minority, soon to be outnumbered by the Latins alone. Broadway is a lady of Spain and behind her are the hardy heirs to peasant Mexican blood. Many are illegal aliens who scratch out an insecure income in the hundreds of sweatshops that make everything from cheap discount clothes to fashionable designer goods. These are people who remain nameless when the labels go on the finished products and who often remain penniless when the shop goes out of business.

This is exactly what happened to Elena and thirteen other illegal immigrants who spent two weeks working for a woman named Maria Enriquez, and then were locked out of her shop when the work was done, without getting paid. They were seeking help at an office marked with the imposing title: Concentrated Enforcement Program, Division of Labor Standards Enforcement, Department of Industrial Relations, State of California.

Behind the sign in a back room down the hall sat Joe Razo. He listened to their story and then sent a team of inspectors over to the closed shop. At first they were told that the owner wasn't there, but when they returned with one of the workers who had been closed out, Maria Enriquez was identified and arrested. She had collected all of the profits from her contract work for a clothing manufacturer, locked out the fourteen people who had worked for her, and flown to Mexico to spend $3,000 on her daughter's wedding. She had returned and was looking to open up shop again in the same place.

"Since our office opened two years ago," recounted Joe Razo, "we've filed 157 criminal complaints, got convictions in all but five cases and sent twenty offenders to jail. We're eliminating the chronic violater from the industry."

Joe makes his preference abundantly clear: he is less concerned with the illegality of a person's status in this country than he is with the illegal abuse these people suffer within our borders. "We don't cooperate, and have no contact, with the Immigration and Naturalization Service. That was one of the stipulations I gave when I took this job."

"Three months ago we were filing criminal charges against an employer, and the lawyer for the contractor asked our witness if she was in the country with legal documentation. She said no. He then said he would have her deported and called the INS. I called the media. Reporters came right to the court. There was no way we would let our witness be deported. Neither we nor the INS are in business to pick up individuals, but rather to stop the exploitation of people.

"In my San Diego office, I remember helping two Guatemalans who had been beaten by a farmer who had hired them. The hospital called the INS when they found they were here illegally. The Guatemalans were already at the INS office when we got there. We got them released into our custody and we filed criminal charges against the employer."

Razo no longer concentrates on farmworkers, although there are many illegal immigrants in the field. His work now is centered in the cities, picking up violators of the labor laws. "We've collected $4.5 million from employers for back pay due to alien workers in garment shops and restaurants. We hold the money for six months while we try to trace the unpaid or underpaid employees, 40 percent of whom we never find. The money then goes to a trust fund for seven years, from which the entitled workers can still take their claims. After that the funds become part of the state treasury."

Besides the money, his office also collects much of the product that has been illegally produced. His office is filled with dresses and gigantic piles of plastic bags stuffed with confiscated fabric. New York leads the nation in the production of men's wear, but Los Angeles is the center of the women's apparel industry. It is now growing at three times the rate of New York and by the end of the century many feel that Los Angeles will be the center for the entire clothing business.

"We have close to a million dollars worth of clothes here," Razo disclosed, showing J.C. Penny and other popular labels. "What happens is this: a retail store, like Penny's, will determine what's selling and order the item by the thousands from a designer through a contract with the manufacturer. The designer draws the pattern, then sends it to the cutter, who cuts the cloth. Finally, the manufacturer makes a deal with a contractor to get the clothes sewn properly but cheaply. The contractor hires the cheapest labor he or she can find. Four out of five of these workers will be women. Four out of five will also be aliens, and therefore four out of five will not be paid the minimum wage or overtime. The employee and the aliens always get the shaft.

"This morning about fifty employees came in here because their employer had not paid them. We filed a preferred claim for them, so that if there is any money returned in bankruptcy proceedings, they will get paid first. In any case, it would take up to six months to process the claim which is an impossible time for people who are already impoverished. This is what we have to deal with three or four times a week. It happens daily. It happened the day before Christmas. A group of garment workers came in here with checks marked 'insufficient funds.' We found people on Labor Day working and they hadn't even punched in.

"In the first six months our office was open, we did 842 inspections, almost all of them unannounced, and found violations of the labor laws and the rights of workers in 96 percent of the shops. The percentage of violations has dropped down about one percent every month to under 80 percent as the word got out that we were around and we were serious. Yet, whether it's the U.S. Department of Labor, the INS, or us trying to enforce the standards, we are all fighting a trench war with hand-to-hand combat. All we have is a finger in the dyke until we can come up with a comprehensive national policy on immigration and labor.

"One policy is that declared by the Statue of Liberty. We will accept all the political and economic refugees who come or who are sent to us. The other is typified by the agribusiness position of the Southwest—we need the cheapest labor we can get. We don't want their children; we only want their sweat. We want those willing to take jobs and salaries the U.S. citizens, even resident aliens, will not accept. This is like the policy of Europe where Germany is bringing in more than two million foreign workers at one time. Get their sweat, then get them the hell out.

"Employer sanctions will not stop exploitation of undocumented workers. All the employer has to do under the law is to make a reasonable attempt to determine that the worker is here legally. It is easy to fraudulently duplicate the green cards that declare the bearer the right to work as a U.S. resident. An employer alone cannot discover whether or not a person is here legally. Due to the maze of immigration law, not even the attorneys specializing in immigration now seem able to determine the legal status of the nation's many new arrivals.

"I've conducted enough voter registration in East Los Angeles to know that behind every other door is an illegal resident. There are certainly more than a million, maybe up to 12 million undocumented people in the United States. If we do not declare amnesty for them and their families, then we are dividing rather than unifying families, which is the commonly stated goal of the religious and Hispanic communities and of the Immigration and Naturalization Service."

Homework

Child labor and sweatshop exploitation did not stop with the passage of the labor laws in this country. "We still find fourteen-year-olds working illegally, at least in the restaurants. Here in Beverly Hills and Hollywood all the cooks and restaurant help are aliens. We collected half a million dollars from Sambo's Restaurants alone for unpaid wages. But when it comes to the sweatshops, it's a different story. We don't even know where the new ones are. You can go to City Hall and get a license for $26, buy or rent some sewing machines, set up shop, exploit some workers, close down and move on, and never get caught. Unless every damn state has the same diligence we have here, then what we're doing won't make any difference."

If anywhere, the movement seems to be in the opposite direction. In New York, the State Labor Department's budget was cut by 40 percent, terminating the unannounced investigations of the garment industry that had been the cornerstone of the Division of Labor Standards' enforcement since the early 1930s. Now inspections occur only in response to employee complaints, giving sweatshop operators the time and freedom to move anywhere they want.

One group of undocumented women went to the New York offices of the International Ladies Garment Workers Union to get help in their grievances against the owner of a non-union shop. They had labored in it for weeks at fifteen dollars for a sixteen-hour day, after which their paychecks were returned stamped insufficient funds. When they asked their employer for their pay, he said he would pay only if they produced their green cards. Fearing deportation, they dropped their complaints and changed their addresses the same night. Most have certainly moved on to other sweatshops where a similar scene is likely to be played. Meanwhile, all manner of federal and state agencies juggle wage, health, and safety standards and try to come up with something that is workable. At the same time, the waiting list for green card applications at the INS stretches to two years and beyond.

In California, the sweatshop operators try to outmaneuver officials like Joe Razo in increasingly clever ways. One is the institution of homework. In this scheme, the operators send their workers home with piles of clothing to sew, and pay them five dollars a day instead of the legal minimum of $3.10 an hour. Probably 10 percent of the clothes now produced in California are being done as homework. "I saw a sign on the front porch of a private home that read: 'We need operators," recounted Razo. "I watched it on my way to and from work and found that there were six operators sewing in a converted garage out back. So we're getting ready to move in and pick them up. You see, minorities, especially Hispanics, have a high rate of carrying tuberculosis. The fumes from the cloth, the roaches and other such unsanitary and unsafe conditions make it unacceptable to allow homework."

This is why Joe fought for a tough law against this sort of practice in the garment industry. The federal law prohibits homework for all except the handicapped, and the California law does this one better by allowing for the confiscation of all fabric and finished products in the hands of homeworkers.

"We have jurisdiction now only over employer-employee relations. We can deal with violations by contractors. Yet it's the manufacturers of clothes who set the prices and the structure. The prices manufacturers give to the contractors aren't sufficient to pay the employees the minimum wage, workers compensation and other benefits. So we can't just go after the small fish. We have to drag the manufacturer into the net, filing negligence charges if the clothes are improperly or unsafely produced, or if they are taken home by the workers."

In July 1981, the new state law mentioned before will officially go into effect. It requires contractors and manufacturers to register with the Division of Labor Standards Enforcement. "If we find that either the contractor or the manufacturer is not registered, by law we must confiscate the clothing. The purpose is to make a manufacturer certain that his contractor is reliable and registered, instead of just shopping around for the cheapest contract available. On the first violation we will not only charge them for the back pay due employees but also fine them $50 per employee. A second violation will draw a $100 per worker and a third will lead to revocation of registration.

"Here is another situation we hope to correct: A manufacturer checks clothes made by the contractor, testing for quality control. If they are not properly made, the clothes may be sent by the manufacturer to a second contractor to be finished or refinished. The new cost is then deducted from the payment to the first contractor, who will then take the loss out of his employee's pay. Then the only recourse is to take the manufacturer to civil court for breach of contract. If you are lucky, the case will be heard in three or four years and it will cost more in court fees than what you'll get if you win. So we got a provision in the new law for mandatory arbitration on quality control disputes between contractors and manufacturers.

"State law is just our first line of defense. If the state law fails, we go to criminal law. If that fails, we turn to legislation to restructure the industry. Our fourth line is to bring in the media to focus attention on the problem or violation. And our last, but by no means least, is to establish cooperation with community and religious groups concerned with defending the rights of workers.

Shop on Broadway

Many of the illegal operations with which Joe Razo has to deal are situated right in his own neighborhood. Downtown Los Angeles abounds with small sewing shops tucked into the corners of old buildings. Looking through Razo's inspection file, I found the address of a past violator and walked down Broadway to see for myself what the working conditions were like. When I arrived at the appropriate number I looked at the directory and found alongside many Asian and Latin names, a small thumb-tacked invitation: "Operadoras con experiencia—experienced operators."

I walked up the stairs, down a drab hall with cracked plaster and water stains everywhere and found room after room of women crowded next to sewing machines. They were leaning forward on hard metal folding chairs and working at a furious pace. Few noticed my camera as I walked past the open doors but those who did, cowered or hid. Some of the overseers shut the door in my face but others were left open. These rooms were so small and packed so high with clothes that I'm sure the door couldn't swing. As I stood there I realized just how impossibly trapped these people are. They need jobs and have them but the cost is so appalling. What is their alternative? If they complain, they will lose their jobs. The operators can easily close down and move to another address, another state, or even another country. These sweatshops are some of the few places where American business is taking in more workers and expanding the labor pool. For an illegal alien who is afraid of deportation the choices are few. These people will talk to no one.

Later that week I had an opportunity to talk with a woman who was working illegally in the garment industry. Even with a reference and recommendation from the church, our meeting never came off. When I went to her house, two young children appeared and told me she was out. I offered to wait, but they said they didn't know when she would return. I went away for a few hours and then came back. Again, through a small crack in the door, I was told she wasn't home.

"Many undocumented aliens look at a job here as their last chance to climb out of poverty and a hopeless life, and a last chance to bring their families out of it too," said George Montoya, chief of general investigations for the INS in New York. "You feel like you are taking their last hope away when you find them."

The Cost of Sweat

"There was little hope to make a better life in Guaymas, the city in Mexico where I was raised," reflected Lola. "My

family was very poor. We had to quit school to help my
·mother sell paper flowers and chewing gum to tourists. I was
married when I was fifteen. As a mechanic, my husband was
able to support my mother with a few pesos a month. When I
was seventeen we moved to Los Angeles. Here you have an
opportunity for a better life, even if you are a poor person. In
Mexico, once you are poor, you die poor."

Patricia, another illegal garment worker, explained how
she came to work in the sweatshops of Los Angeles. "It was
my widowed mother who first went to the United States to
work. She would send money to my poor grandparents who
took care of me. They didn't have enough money to care for
me. They had no pension plan or social security. Then my
mother wrote saying she could get me a job in Los Angeles
and I could live with her. I took a bus from Toluca to Tijuana
where I met my mother and her friend, a legal U.S. resident
who worked in the same shop with her. She drove us across
the border in her Chevrolet and my mother got me a job in the
same sweatshop she worked in."

These people keep coming and the same stories are
repeated. The desperate flight from poverty forces them to
take any job at any pay. Such willingness to work makes
many people in this country antagonistic, thinking the aliens
are taking jobs and money from them. But experts on immigration and labor like Wayne Cornelius at the University of
California at San Diego argue that there is little evidence to
suggest this. "We have found that immigrants often put more
into the system than they get from it," he said. "For obvious
reasons many of them do not take advantage of tax-funded
programs, although they are taxpayers."

An extensive study of apprehended aliens by the U.S.
Department of Labor found that over 75 percent of them held
unskilled or semi-skilled jobs, with the vast majority getting
wages far below the level acceptable to U.S. residents. Only
1.6 percent worked as professionals or in technical jobs and

only 15.5 percent in crafts. Therefore few would be in direct economic competition with native U.S. workers.

Furthermore, most do not come to stay. They are only temporary residents for a few months, a harvest season, or a couple of years before they return to their families in Mexico. But no matter how long they stay, they tend to leave more than they take. The Labor Department study found that only 5 percent of the apprehended aliens had made use of available medical care; 3.9 percent had received unemployment benefits; 1.3 percent had received food stamps, and less than one percent had obtained any welfare payments.

Yet every study found that 75 percent had federal income and Social Security taxes withheld from their paychecks. They also rarely file tax returns to be eligible for refunds or stay in the country long enough to qualify for Social Security. The Department of Labor also found that less than .4 percent had children enrolled in school.

Like many who have come before, today's undocumented workers face a life dependent on the domestic economy and the mood of American people and politicians. From World War II through 1964 as many as half a million Mexican nationals were allowed into the U.S. in a single year to work in agriculture under a contract negotiated between the U.S. Department of Labor, growers associations and the Mexican government. They were brought in at wages the U.S. workers would not accept. They lived in company camps. They ate from company stores and they were regularly returned to Mexico if they complained or tried to organize. Even though this system was stopped, still about 20,000 foreign workers each year are given temporary visas to come to the U.S. and work the fields of New England, Virginia, Florida, and Texas. These aliens can easily be denied their full rights and protection under the law, and at the same time be used to replace or demoralize domestic workers who will not accept such mistreatment.

"We must look not only at the economic but also the moral base of immigration," said Frank Galvan, immigration program coordinator for the American Friends Service Committee in Los Angeles. "In times of economic disparity, the nation looks for a scapegoat. It is time for religious people to be reminded that we are a pilgrim people, that we look at these strangers as our brothers and sisters in faith. The unsettled and undocumented people are the constituency of no one. We can offer them services that the government can't or won't."

"Since they do not vote, the politicians do not come to their aid," said Joe Razo. "They must rely on people outside of the government to work on their behalf, whether they be in community organizations or in religious denominations. Half of the clothes you are wearing right now were manufactured in sweatshops or as homework. It took the worker an hour to sew your shirt or blouse, for which that person received maybe a dollar. Rather than wait for the state or federal government to initiate some innovative procedures, I will work for the strict enforcement of the present legal safeguards and I will continue to ask everyone—in the community, in the churches and synagogues—to expose, boycott, oppose and finally close down all those who exploit the defenseless alien workers."

Joe is right. The poverty they suffer is in part the basis of the prosperity we all enjoy. Many of these people have already returned to their homes in Mexico. But to those that remain, their health and their hope as well as their jobs are in our hands. We must give them their full measure of human rights as long as they are on our soil. If they ask of us as they asked of Mexico, "Dame la bendicion de tu poderosa mano —Give me the blessing of your powerful hand," it is ours to respond, "Te llevo en mi corazon—I take you in my heart."

CHAPTER 6

Adriana:

In the House of Torture

Mírame desde el fondo de la tierra, . . .
aguador de las lágrimas andinas,
joyero de los dedos machacados,
agricultor temblando en la semilla,
alfarero en tu greda derramado:
traed a la copa de esta nueva vida
vuestros viejos dolores enterrados.
Mostradme vuestra sangre y vuestro surco;
decidme: aquí fui castigado
porque la joya no brilló o la tierra
no entregó a teimpo la piedra o el grano.
Señaladme la piedra en que caísteis,
y la madera en que os crucificaron.
Encendédme los viejos pedernales
las viejas lámparas, los látigos pegados
a través de los siglos en las llagas
y las hachas de brillo ensangrentade. . . .

Contadme todo, cadena a cadena,
eslabón a eslabón, y paso a paso;
afilad los cuchillos que guardasteis,
ponedlos en mi pecho y en mi mano,
como un río de rayos amarillos,
como un río de tigres enterrados,
y dejadme llorar: horas, días, años,
edades ciegas, siglos estelares.

Dadme el silencio, el agua, la esperanza.

Dadme la lucha, el hierro, los volcanes.

Apegadme los cuerpos como imanes.

Acudid a mis venas y a mi boca.

Hablad por mis palabras y sangre.

Look at me from the depths of the earth, . . .
iceman of Andean tears,
jeweler with crushed fingers,
farmer anxious among his seedlings,
potter wasted among his clays:
bring to the cup of this new life
your ancient buried sorrows.
Show me your blood and your furrow;
say to me: here I was scourged
because a gem was dull or the earth
failed to give up in time its tithe of stone or corn.
Point out to me the rock on which you stumbled,
the wood they used to crucify your body.
Strike the old flints

to kindle ancient lamps, light up the whips
glued to your wounds throughout the centuries
and light the axes gleaming with your blood....
And tell me everything, tell chain by chain,
and link by link, and step by step;
sharpen the knives you kept hidden away,
thrust them into my breast, into my hands,
like a torrent of sunbursts,
an Amazon of buried jaguars,
and let me cry; hours, days, years.
blind ages, stellar centuries.

And give me silence, water, hope.

Give me the struggle, the iron, the volcanoes.

Let bodies cling like magnets to my body.

Come quickly to my veins and to my mouth.

Speak through my speech and blood.

She can show no portrait. Even her passport photo cannot be seen by strangers. She lives in the danger of discovery and in the brutal confines of her own memory. She is a woman without a country, a mother without a son. These lines from a poem by Pablo Neruda act like an invocation as her image emerges from sorrow and shadow.

Adriana. Her last name remains hidden, bound by blood to her son who remains in a Chilean cell. She now lives in Chicago. But she is less an immigrant than an exile. She is less a pilgrim than an expatriot. She does not speak of the American dream but of a Chilean nightmare with American ghosts. Her story goes from prison to prison. Her words tear at the terror. This is the story of both her liberation and loss.

Las Visitas

Adriana was born in Los Andes and grew up in the great port of Valparaiso. She was the daughter of an army sergeant and the granddaughter of a shipbuilder. She remembers her childhood in Chile as a graceful time filled with strong ships, soft gardens, tea and chocolate.

"There was a pretty forest with gardens and flowers," she recalled. "There was also a church at La Nani where we would worship on Sundays. When they had dances and festivities, they would give me chocolate.

"Grandpa built us a place where we could play Las Visitas—Visitors. The older girls were the visitors and it was for the youngest to be the good hostess. I was the youngest. We would serve and drink tea, walk and play in the garden, and dream of marrying a military man like my grandfather. He had no vices. He was perfect, so I thought everyone in the military was a good person. Only later did I see that he was what he was because of himself, not because of the military. When I was a child, we also played the game of torture. We tied victims to trees. It was only a game then."

House of Torture

By 1975, a U.S.-backed military coup had overthrown the elected Chilean government of Salvador Allende Gossens. Afterwards, dissent was prohibited and meetings were forbidden. Adriana lived near the University of Santiago at the time, with her only child, Juan. "We lived in a house where we had a clear view of the street. Crowds were uncommon because no one in Chile was allowed to gather a group in public. People were picked up and disappeared at random. Terror and fear were everywhere. So when I saw a group gathering in the street I went out to investigate. Rumors had spread around the neighborhood that someone was going to get picked up. Outside on the street corner, I overheard the police say that they were looking for someone. I listened to the description. It was my son.

"I went back to the house. Juan was there. So were six of his student friends who had come to defend him when they heard he was in danger of arrest. Soon forty or fifty men in civilian clothes arrived, surrounded the house, and pointed guns at us. They were members of DINA, the only group allowed to carry guns in Chile. They were the national investigation force, trained by the CIA in the United States.

"All eight of us were arrested and blindfolded. My son was accused of being a delinquent, of belonging to a socialist political group. It was September 6, 1975. It was damp and cold, and I was stripped of my heavy jersey and overcoat so that I could feel the chill. On the way to our destination, Juan broke loose from the paddy wagon and, still handcuffed, ran into a large park we were passing. Soon four helicopters were on the scene, pursuing him through the park and the city. He was caught and returned to the wagon.

"In the car with me was a pregnant woman whose husband had already been killed by torture. They had packed up all my books and Juan's, too, in a suitcase. Science, politics, everything. Then they threw the heavy suitcase at this preg-·nant, blindfolded woman and hit her in the stomach. She and her defenseless fetus took the entire blow. A month later, I saw her and she showed me a picture of the baby she was carrying at the time. She told me the child had been born alive, but damaged, and had died within a few days.

"DINA took everything that belonged to Juan, his books and his clothes. They took from me the property I owned where we were going to build a school. They moved into our house to 'guard' it and stayed for over a month and messed up everything. After they left, it was boarded up. They also took rings and necklaces that were handed down in my family for generations. I gave up two golden roses with precious stones in the center, gifts made for me by my students. They even took my family pictures. All I had left was the thin blouse and slacks I was wearing.

"We were going to La Casa de Tortura—The House of Torture. We had heard about it but nobody knew its exact location. When we arrived, though we could not see, we knew where we were. I heard the screams of the young man who had come to our house earlier that day to warn us.

"The first few days, they kept me standing in a yard, sometimes until two in the morning. It was damp and cold because September is the worst time of year in Chile. At night they would take me into an office where several gunmen would yell verbal abuses at me, push me and hold guns to my head. When they took off my blindfold for the first time, I saw that the men who had pushed me and shouted at me were sitting around the room eating and drinking. I had nothing to eat except a bowl of soup once a day.

"There were two other women in the House of Torture when I arrived. One was accused of carrying messages like some sort of informer and the other was a young nurse whose only crime was that she worked among the poor. In Chile, even that is seen as a threat to the state. I saw the nurse later in a concentration camp but I never saw the other woman again.

"One night they took me out of the prison blindfolded and forced me to take them to my brother. I took them to my brother's place because I knew he wasn't political. When we got to the housing project, they took off my blindfold and I could see all the DINA carabineros stooped down pointing guns toward the building. After I had led them to my brother's apartment door, they took me away and I didn't find out until a month later what happened, when they allowed my mother to visit me. She said they broke into the apartment, searched the place, beat up my brother and then left.

"Finally they took me to a room in the prison that looked like an old kitchen. It was cold and damp and bare. I stayed there all the time after that, except whenever they forced me to stand in the yard. When I touched the sink, I received an electric shock. They had the cell wired and seemed to be able to change the amount of current running through things depending on what they wanted to do. Sometimes it was stronger than other times.

"At first I couldn't sleep. I began to think that I could feel the current running through me all the time. But after awhile I got used to it and could even stand the current long enough to get a drink of water. There was no furniture, no bed and no blanket. All I had were the thin clothes I wore.

"After a few days I began to notice that I could hear someone breathing in the room next to me. Then I realized it was my son. I had taught yoga and I knew the sound of his breath very well. The next night I heard them beating him, but he wasn't saying anything. Suddenly my door opened and someone came in, struck me, grabbed my hair, and dragged me over to the next cell where they were keeping my son. They had his hands tied behind him, and they sat me down in front of him. They began punching me with fists like hammers in my temples and asking over and over, "Is this your son?" But I didn't say anything. Finally Juan said, 'Yes, I am.' Then they took me back to my cell and left.

"Two weeks later my son was taken to another room, hung naked with his hands tied behind his back, and whipped up and down the entire length of his body. He now has scars from his legs up to his head. After that they put him in a chair that was all metal and put an adjustable metal collar around his neck. They took me there and I had to watch them charge him with electricity, shock after shock, until he lost consciousness.

"On September 29, they told me that I could see him on the one condition that I wouldn't cry or make a fuss. I agreed. When I saw him they had him all dressed up and clean, but he looked stiff and he turned his head with difficulty. His eyes were red and hazy and could only stare blankly around the room. They told me he was insane and would never be the same again. But when he saw me, he recognized me and said to me softly, 'Mama, why do you worry? We knew what we would have to go through.'

"For a long time I only saw him through a crack in my window when they would take him to the bathroom. Then in October, they started taking us out to the yard for ten minutes of sun. There we could talk, though we were always under guard. He told me they allowed him to exercise, and I saw him begin to recuperate. By the end of the month he reached a point where he could understand quite well.

"Meanwhile we all struggled to keep up our strength. We were still only getting a bowl of soup once a day. I noticed some small grapevines running along the wall. Although they bore no grapes, we soon learned that the leaves were edible, and we shared those. The taller prisoners would reach up and break them off for the rest of us.

"One November morning at five o'clock, eight of us were taken out into the darkness and driven away," Adriana continued. "I heard someone say that they were going to take our passports and dump us into Argentina. I knew of a large group who had been taken to the border before. There they had been abandoned and then killed by the Argentinian border patrol. I really thought it was going to be the end of us."

Instead they were transported to a Chilean concentration camp called Tres Alamos. There Adriana was given a room with a bed and a bowl of beans. "I could not swallow the beans but I was forced to eat them. It took me almost the whole day to get them down. They had given us nothing to drink." Within a day she was given a roommate who had been arrested because she had climbed a hill to post a flag of the revolutionary movement just as the police happened by. Then another woman came, a Christian Democrat, who was arrested because she stuck out her tongue at the wife of dictator Augusto Pinochet.

"More than five hundred women came and went from my room during the month I was there. Students, social workers, laborers, housewives. Only one woman, a doctor, remained the whole time I was there. Once I remember that a pregnant woman was brought into our room. We were still getting mostly soup broth, but whenever something more substantial was in our bowls, we would take it out and give it to that woman.

"Suddenly one day, they came and took me from the room and into the hallway. There I saw some of the people who had been with me when I was tortured. They put a mask on me, tied my hands together and then tied them to one of my ankles. Then they tied me to the leg of someone who was bound in the same way. They made us walk, tied together like that. He was nearly dragging me along the ground, but I didn't make a sound. I didn't want him to know it was me. He was my son.

"As Juan was climbing into the car, I fell and hurt myself, and someone picked me up and threw me in on top of him. It was then that I felt that he knew who it was. But he didn't say a thing.

"We rode silently up a mountain. I could hear airplanes. Then we stopped and were taken out and walked through the woods. Through my mask I could see a body lying on the ground in front of a wooden cabin. A man was taken inside and another body was brought out and thrown down beside me. Then they took my son into the cabin and while he was in there I heard him screaming, 'Not my mother!' When he came out we were tied together again but now he was very weak. He was leaning on me and he kept fainting, his head falling on my chest.

"When we came down from the mountain, they separated us and took me back to the place I had first been tortured.

There my hands were tied behind my back and I was beaten all over my body. It is terrible to have your hands tied behind you like that. When I was untied, I could not move my arms to the front. I still have the scars from the handcuffs, a painful back, nauseous stomach and throbbing headaches."

Free Speech

On December 10, Adriana was moved to Libre Platica— Free Speech, another section of Tres Alamos. Though far from 'free' in any real sense of the word, it was freer. "When I walked into Free Speech," she reflected, "at least a hundred women recognized me from our past miseries and rushed up and kissed me and sang to me. They told me, 'Here we are all united. They won't do anything more to you.' Besides, they had nothing to worry about, we were all so sick that no one even thought of escaping. So we organized ourselves to make the best society we could right where we were. The only thing the prison system provided was soup, so we set about meeting our other needs. Families could visit, and so we had them bring in as much food as we needed. Then we asked visitors to bring in books, and we started our own library. Anybody who had a skill gathered a group and taught it. I started one for yoga.

"It was like a co-op. We shared everything. When someone new came in, she got clothing, soap, food, and anything special we could provide. Among our people we could make anything from soup to shoes. I taught the sick women how to breathe deeply so they could develop and hold their strength. There were about 500 of us there. Each with something important to contribute to the strength of the whole.

"One day a Bible was brought in and we hid it and passed it around," Adriana remembered. She also recalled the day when the priest assigned by the government to preach there gave his first Mass. "About forty of us women went to hear him. He said, 'Let us pray so that God can forgive you for the sins you have committed, so that you may repent for all you have done.' He could not continue. All of us stood up and walked out. The next Sunday, nobody went, so he came down to see us, wondering what was wrong. One woman told him, 'You started off wrong. We are not the ones to repent. It is you and the system you represent that are killing and torturing the people.' The only thing that priest could say was, 'I am only doing what I was told.'"

Familiar Faces

In 1976, shortly after she was released from Free Speech, Adriana was given the chance to leave Chile, and she took it. Her visa came through quickly, and her plane ticket was paid for by the Methodist church in Illinois that agreed to sponsor her immigration. "I came to the United States not because I wanted to come, but because, my family and friends thought that if I did my son wouldn't have to suffer anymore. I chose this country because at the time, other countries would have taken longer. I came here to get away from the intimidation, but I'm beginning to think that it's hopeless.

"On the plane that was bringing me here I was shocked to see faces that I recognized from when I was being tortured. One of the men who had beaten me was sitting just across the aisle. They might have been coming to this country to take part in the assassination of Chilean ambassador Letelier who was killed just four months after I arrived. Since I have been here, my life has also been threatened.

"The first time I took a train in Chicago," Adriana stated, "I saw another man who had tortured me in Chile. He got on at the same stop as me and got off when I got off. Four different times when I was leaving college on Wabash

Avenue, the same coffee-colored car rushed by and tried to run me down. The same car passed my house many times. One morning as I came up to the bus stop to go to work, that car passed by and stopped right where the bus was supposed to stop. The bus came and pulled up in front of him. I didn't know what to do. I was afraid to cross the street, thinking he might try to run me down, but I was afraid not to cross, worried that if the bus left, I would be alone on the street. So as the bus door opened I hurried across the street. Just as I was getting on the bus, the car pulled out and nearly hit me."

Reticent Alien

She clutches her purse stuffed with the wrinkled papers of her past. There are letters from family and friends, scraps of her own poetry, and the frayed pages of her son's defense. In many ways this is all she has left, and she will not leave them in her apartment for fear they will be stolen. She lives more in transit than in place. Her face is only dimly related to the photo that is attached to her five-year-old passport. The only thing new in her bag is the crisp green card from the INS that grants her the legal right to work.

"I got it last October," she said as she stuck the card back in her wallet. "I have not been well enough to work much anyway. I have been sick most of the time since I have been here. Last year I wanted to go to a conference in England and tell them about my son but I couldn't go because I didn't have the card yet. Even though they said in 1978 that it would only take two months for Chileans, it took me two years to get mine."

Adriana pulled out the text of her son's defense and paged through it. He is still in jail, his sixth year, awaiting a hearing in his defense that has been prepared by a lawyer provided by the Catholic Church. She rehearsed the charges and added her own testimony. "My son says yes, he is a member of a political party, that he does not go back on his word and commitment because he knows his responsibility to his country. But he also says that he never participated in any negative political action and that if he admitted to doing so, it was only because he was being tortured and was trying to protect his mother. This case has been in process for five years. If the United States wanted to, it could get my son out right away because it was this country, through the CIA, that got all of us into trouble in the first place. They are the ones who trained the secret police and backed the brutal regime that now has my son imprisoned.

"You know I have no power here, no power to vote or to affect the system. If the U.S. does not allow me into its politics, then the U.S. should not become involved in the politics of my country. Years ago, your banks gave millions of dollars to Chile, money with which the junta bought all the arms and everything else it needed to terrorize the people.

"Under Allende, the university and books were free to all those who would learn. With the new government, a third of the students had to leave because they couldn't afford to pay. Now only the rich can go. This is all done to keep the rich in power and the U.S. benefits as Chile increases its exports."

In spite of all this, Adriana maintains a kind of stubborn strength. Everyday she works in a storefront where she helps newer immigrants find jobs and a sense of community. And she plans for the day when her son will be released. She only admits to her own present difficulties in the most casual way. "It is very hard to gather everything together. I forget things. But maybe that's for the better." She seems to reserve her real passion for others. "There are so many others who faced and passed worse horrors than mine. I must learn to have more courage, and I must say to the others who have suffered as I have, as we all have, keep your sanity till the end."

CHAPTER 7

David Won:

Combat in Boston

What am I looking for? Soul,
my blind soul, endlessly darting
like children at play by the river,
answer me: where am I going?

Flowing like a river moving south, streams of displaced Koreans filled the roads that ran away from the war. The world had been fighting for years by the time David Won was born in 1943 and his country was still under the control of the Japanese. The plea for freedom in the above lines from "Does Spring Come to Stolen Fields?" by Korean poet Yi Samg-Hwa was still unanswered.

By the time David Won was seven there was a new war. This time it was Korean against Korean. By then, 1950, there were few children playing in the village of Sam Dong because few children remained. He was alone in his grandparents' house when the North Koreans slipped over the mountains and into their village. He had been inadvertently left behind when they fled by boat before the battle. There were no men left. No women. Only a few boys remained. David Won was one of them. This is the story of a soul looking, darting between nations.

Seven-year-old David Won was visiting his grandparents in the summer of 1950 when the border broke. Before his eyes, his grandparents' village of Sam Dong that until then had been a serene vacation retreat turned into a battleground on which the future of Korea was to be determined. The war started in June with the advance of the troops from the North who were seeking the reunification of Korea under communist control. By the end of the summer, U.N. forces under the command of General MacArthur had turned back the assault. For the next year, David was caught in the middle as the war went back and forth.

"I woke up early one morning to the sound of guns outside my grandparents' house," David recalled. "I looked outside and saw a lot of people in the road, walking and running to the South. Some lay still along the way, already killed in the attack. Ground transportation stopped. The people fled by whatever means they could, leaving the village of Sam Dong to a dozen of us boys who were left behind.

"I was 200 miles away from my home in Seoul and I had no idea where to go. I was terrified, yet fascinated, when I ran out into the crossfire. I could hear bullets whiz by near my ears. I didn't understand the danger until I began to see people falling dead around me. I darted between the bullets and the houses like a refugee with nowhere to go.

"I ran into Chinese and Korean soldiers and they treated me kindly. Some of them stayed in part of my family's house. They gave me food and gifts and told me about the new united nation that was coming. Then one day I looked out and saw a friend of my grandfather coming up the road. Just as he approached the house, a U.S. plane flew over with its machine gun firing. I ran outside. He was already dead when I reached him." At that time, David Won had no idea that years later he would find himself on another American plane going to start a new life in Boston.

Ambitions

David Won is a survivor who has lived through three wars. He saw the end to Japanese domination of his homeland and he suffered through the Korean War. Then as a soldier in the army of the Republic of Korea, from 1963 to 1966, he went to Vietnam. Fortunately he only had to watch. His duty was playing saxophone in the army band, but he kept his eyes open and learned a lot.

"My brother Ho played trumpet in the Korean Army band, and we both went to Vietnam. We were stationed there with about 40,000 other Korean soldiers. That's where we saw for the first time that Koreans are tougher than Americans. Your soldiers were much more restrained than ours when dealing with the communists. That explains why Korea is now the second strongest country in Asia, after Japan. When we were freed from Japanese control, Korea was very poor. But with U.S. help we kept developing economically and now we are very strong. The U.S. doesn't control us anymore, it just helps us."

Now, for American citizens, there are some hard questions to be faced concerning the kind of help we give Korea. Democracy as we know it is dead in South Korea today. The new martial-law regime of President Chun Doo Hwan is laced with oppression. Under his rule, 172 periodicals have been suspended, 400 journalists have been dismissed, and more than 1,000 civilians were killed during last May's uprising for freedom in Kwangju City.

As far as David Won is concerned, these developments

have to be viewed in context. "Chun has a powerful country. A country's strength and stability is more important than the political system in control. Any system, except communism, is acceptable if it allows for economic freedom and keeps the country strong. If you have a free economy, you can have new ideas for advancement. For a country to survive, it always needs the opportunity and development that such things as new markets provide. That is why the opening of trade between the U.S. and China is such a good idea."

When David was released from the South Korean army he returned to Seoul and began working in the construction business. In the following three years he built twelve houses, married his wife Kong, had two sons and started working in the import-export business. It was in connection with this work that he first came to the United States on a six-month visa. Soon he extended it for six months more, got a working visa and a green card, and in 1974 joined the U.S. Army in Massachusetts and became the only Korean member of any of the army's bands. By 1975 he became a United States citizen.

"For my first three years here, my brother in Seoul would write me and call me on the phone. He was trying to get me to come back, saying they were all worried about me. He told me that Kong and the children needed me and that he wanted me to work in his business. He is still in construction there. I knew it was hard for my wife being alone, not so much financially but personally, raising our boys alone. I could not go back before I was a success here."

As the Koreans say, it was a matter of ch'emyon—face or reputation. Maintaining one's face, losing it, regaining it or even gambling it are deadly serious matters for a Korean. David did not feel he could rejoin his family until he could stand proudly before them.

"I am a man," David continued. "I had to prove I could make it here before I could look back." For his wife and sons, however, looking back was all they could do when they first came here. "When I got to the airport in Boston to pick them up, I thought they hadn't come. I didn't see them anywhere. Then I asked the airline attendant if a Korean woman and two small boys were on the plane. I were told that they went right to the rest rooms to wash their faces before they saw me. It was a beautiful reunion. All we had was pictures to keep us before each other's eyes. Now we were face to face again."

But soon the realities of their new lives began to hit his wife and children. For weeks, David would come home each night and find Kong crying and pleading, "Please take me back to Korea." She was afraid of a culture and language that she couldn't understand. His two sons, Young J. Won and Young N. Won had similar reactions. They had troubles in school and wanted to stay home. One day Young J. came home crying from school. "They gave him homework," David remembered. "But he would not start it. He said he was waiting for me to help him. So I showed him how to use the dictionary. Everything here is in English of course. The boys had little trouble with math and science, but the reading and writing took special effort."

Now his sons are more at home in the United States than they would be in Korea. They find school here is much easier than it was in Korea, and that is the sort of thing that would make any child happy. But one of the things that Young N. likes about this country is less predictable: "I like the United States because so much is so close. In Korea, you have to go to China to meet Chinese people, and then you can't speak the same language. Here you don't have to go far and you have Chinese, Korean and people from many other countries all together and speaking the same language."

Always

Just thirty minutes from their comfortable colonial home in suburban Winchester is Washington Street in downtown

Boston. It is an avenue of X-rated movies, bookstores and bars called the Combat Zone. Here David opened his first American business. The store is called "Always" and in it he sells just about everything under the sun. He has cosmetics, candy, jewelry, hats, wigs, shoes, cigarettes, combs, cards, radios, handbags, sweaters, fans and many other items. Using the business management skills that David learned when he was in the U.S. Army, he became the first Korean to open his own business in Boston. Always was not his last opening. Last year he added Smoke Town and the Jewelry Depot, both nearby, to his small but booming enterprise. He also helped a Korean friend get started.

"One of my friends who played trumpet with me in the Army helped me out when I opened my first store. So last year I helped him with the credit so he could open a place of his own. All my employees are my friends. I like it that way."

David's brother, Ho, also came over from Korea and now works in the shops. It is an arrangement that is good for both of them because of the trust they share. The longer David remains in business in the United States, the more he understands the importance of honesty. To illustrate this he told a story about something that happened during his first year in business. One day he was visited by a man who said he was soliciting for the Policeman's Benevolent Association. In exchange for delivery of a magazine subscription, David gave $150. He never heard from the man, or anyone else, again and never received a single copy of the magazine. According to David that was the last time he was taken by a con man.

David has had other bad experiences in Boston and they are beginning to make him question some of the American values he sees. "I don't know about the United States sometimes," he admitted. "At first I looked at the people and all I saw was smiles. Then I opened my store and every day maybe five people tried to steal from me. I started thinking, wondering why I should be working so hard when someone else can just walk up and take what is mine. I try to work, and others try to take it away. Everybody was kind when I first came here and that was very good. Not now. I see kids with good minds going right from the street to the jail. It's in the economics. When it's hard on people, they get desperate."

Kong voices similar reservations, though she has come a long way from the woman who cried through the first weeks she was here. For the last two years she has had a job in a bindery and has become the best sewer in her section. She recently received a special pay raise for the speed and quality of her work. "I'm thinking I still want to go back to Korea some day. It is bad here between children and parents. There the parents stay in the children's homes. Koreans take care of their parents and give them respect. Here children hide cigarettes from parents, smoke marijuana and do not obey their parents' wishes."

"It is too late for our children to go back to Korea," David concluded. "For their future, it would be better in Korea. The education system is much better there. Their high schools are equal to the junior college level here. But the boys are too much American already. When they have finished school and are on their own, then maybe Kong and I can go back to Korea.

"Of course there are more people here and more of a chance to make money," David continued. "And the people are not so emotional, not so ready to fight as they are in Korea. They are more patient and relaxed. Americans will stand in a long line at a restaurant; Koreans would just leave. Here, I have a lot of freedom, a good standard of living, and I can travel where I want. But sometimes I think Americans have too much freedom. People are more concerned with pets than with other people. I see people steal something, get caught by the police and the next day they are out doing the same thing. A good curfew like in Korea would get the criminals off the streets. In Korea there are the same kind of laws as here, but there they are enforced. I'm thinking of going back to Korea. I'm thinking I made a mistake."

CHAPTER 8

Wood Chuen Kwong:

Canton to Chinatown

From thousands of miles away the wind would
Sweep over the sighs of a distant country:
We have traveled over numerous rivers and hills,
Staying with them for a moment,
   but leaving them all the time.

We are like birds that soar in the sky,
And control the space any time and all the time,
And yet all the time feel totally dispossessed.

What is this thing called our reality?
Nothing can be brought over from afar, and
Nothing can be taken away from here either.

The fleeting movement so beautifully expressed in this verse from Chinese poet Feng Chih bears all of us, sometimes, away like soaring birds. But his question about what it is we take with us and what we leave behind as we move from place to space is surely more poignant for the recent immigrant.

In June of 1979, Wood Chuen Kwong left his home in Canton, China, and came to San Francisco. He came because his mother had died the fall before, and his father was beginning to falter. In November of the same year, his father died in San Francisco and Wood decided to stay on. The things he couldn't bring with him when he came, and those he can't take back if he returns, are at the heart of his story.

Electric Land

"I wouldn't leave Chinatown, even if I were offered a job somewhere else," said Wood Chuen Kwong from his apartment in the heart of the world's largest Chinese community outside of Asia. This city is wonderfully textured with the Chinese sensibility. Graceful calligraphy blinks brilliantly from neon signs on banks, fish markets and boutiques. The Chinese language is spoken at every turn and other aspects of Chinese culture are seen everywhere. Chinatown is like a haven between hemispheres, an oasis of the Orient firmly planted on our western shore.

"I wanted to stay in San Francisco for a year or two, to get acquainted, to get to know the people here. It is such a beautiful city and the weather is wonderful. But it is very difficult to find a job." For now, Wood and his son, Ching Yu, work as dishwashers and busboys, but they hope this is only temporary. Wood is a mechanical engineer and has an extensive background in electronics.

"In Canton, I was a radio repairman for thirty-two years in my spare time. The locally made radios and parts were easy to come by in China, and we always saved any extra parts. In America I see people who are so wasteful. They will throw out a radio if a single part breaks down. All these electric gadgets you have here are luxuries you don't need. We had to cook in China on a messy coal stove. It would be very helpful to have what you have here, the Japanese-made electric frying pans, rice cookers and toasters. But there the people couldn't afford them even if they were available. Here you have useless electric razors and toothbrushes too.

"In Canton our whole family was allowed only 10 kilowatts of electricity each month. One 40-watt lightbulb and one 60-watt fan were all we could afford. All our work and reading had to be done by that one bulb. We also had one three-watt fluorescent lamp we could put in the socket for dim and minimal lighting. There was, of course, no air-conditioning in our apartment, or anywhere else in Canton, even though the heat hit 90 degrees in the autumn and 100 degrees in the summer.

"Living in China, you have to learn how to fix almost anything and everything in your household. For others to fix what you have would take too long and cost too much. So I learned carpentry and began to make tables and chairs. If a leg on something broke, or our bed broke down, I had to fix it. Soon I had repaired a whole house. So did all the other workers that I knew who got about $40 a month for their normal labors.

"All the people were willing to help. If you needed to move something or paint a wall, you could just call on your friends and they would all come and give you a hand to do anything or go anywhere. And they didn't need to be paid." It is just this sort of cooperation between people that Wood finds to be lacking in the United States. Even though he and his wife, Foong Ying Dang, and their son, Ching Yu, and daughter, Ming Yu, feel relatively secure within the cultural haven of Chinatown, they know that they are now living in more threatening surroundings. Rival Chinese street gangs have been trying to assert their dominance, and their presence breeds fear in the new and old residents alike.

"I would not come home late at night, or go out of China-town," admitted Wood. "I have never had any trouble, but I don't feel safe. In China I knew everybody who lived on our block, but here, even people in the same building don't say hello. There may not be enough freedom in China but there is too much here. They have far less crime, very little theft or murder, because the offender in China is handled much more thoroughly and properly. Picking someone's pocket there would get you twenty days to three months in jail. Burglary draws at least two years, armed robbery is ten to twenty years. Murder is for life, with no probation. When the rule and punishment are straight and strong, then you can have restraint. There is no gambling in China because the people don't have the greed that makes them want to take what doesn't belong to them instead of earning it themselves."

Wood takes pride in being able to earn what his family needs though he has known disappointment along these lines and understands that fairness and justice are not always available to everyone. "For about eight years in the 1950s I took part in a Chinese government-promoted plan to provide housing, employment and services. We put our money in the bank, and with the interest the government built homes and left the principle in the bank for future investment. No one person in China could build or afford to buy a house. So the money made some housing available. And each new year we drew lots and several people won the houses. The Cultural Revolution wiped this out before I could win my house. But you know, if the savings and loans in San Francisco would follow that scheme, there would be lots of investors and we could both build houses and provide employment for people in the process."

Wood can see that there is good and bad in both countries. He knows that China could certainly use some American technology and suspects that the U.S. would do well to have more of the will and spirit that the Chinese worker has.

"Opening trade has been and will continue to be beneficial to both the U.S. and China. If China doesn't look to the U.S. for technical progress it will never catch up to the new and better ways that the world can work. And if the U.S. doesn't meet the real spirit of the Chinese people, it will never get out of its old red-devil fear. We are different, but each of us has good points and weaknesses. If we come together we can learn to compliment each other."

Forging Ahead

"I just finished a manpower training program in the Chinatown Resources Development Center and I have already had several interviews for jobs. I've just applied and taken a written examination in English for a government position that I have high hopes for. It is a civil service mechanical technician at $800 a month."

In Canton he made much less money, $113 a month, but his expenses were much less too. His food cost about $10 a month and his rent, for a three-bedroom apartment, was $13.49 a month. He was not dissatisfied with his life there and though he applied for a visa to come here for six years, he only wanted to visit and to see his parents. However the Chinese government refused his requests. Finally his father's influence made the difference.

"My father had studied at Ohio State University before spending his life teaching, first in Canton and then from 1946 to 1968 in Hong Kong. In 1952 one of my sisters and her husband came to the United States. In 1968, my parents followed after my sister's petition for reunification was accepted. None of the rest of us seven children could come out of China with them then.

"In 1979 my father petitioned for me to come out because of the special case of his illness. He was also a commissioner on the housing authority in San Francisco, so through his connections, my case was expedited. I was able to come and be with him before he died. It had been so difficult to get out of China just for a visit that I decided that once I came here I would want to stay. I am now a permanent resident alien. I think I'll decide after five years whether I want to become a U.S. citizen."

Meanwhile one of his sisters has no such choice. She is now a permanent resident alien in a country she doesn't want to be in. She came out of China to Hong Kong at the same time that Wood flew to San Francisco to be with his father. "Father also petitioned for Kin. But when she came out of China in June of 1979, a lot of other people were going to Hong Kong to be processed for America. So the U.S. consulate just listed people in the order of the requests for immigration. She was put way back on the list. When our father died, so did his petition for Kin. The case was closed. Now she cannot come to America nor can she go back to China.

"Kin was a doctor in China, but she can't get recognized in Hong Kong, so she works as an aid in a school for the blind. Her husband was an X-ray specialist in China, but he can't find a job in Hong Kong. They have a very difficult life now. I don't know who is to blame. I often write to her and send money to help. I don't know what else to do."

"Before I arrived here," Wood said, as he changed the subject, "I hoped only to be with my father and to find a job that would allow me enough to support my family. But when I got here and started to study I realized that I have skills to utilize beyond being a dishwasher. In China, I was the twelfth highest employee in a plant with 6,000 workers. I was satisfied with what I had to do and what I did. But I was not satisfied by the lack of long-range planning and followup. Many things I accomplished they later just discarded."

Wood also resented the limits he felt imposed upon his religious expression. "Communism doesn't go hand in hand with Christianity. But in China, during this last generation, we were allowed a little freedom of religion. Then the Cultural Revolution worked to wipe out everything religious. The Moslems were the first to reemerge. Now the Christians are doing the same thing. For thirteen years we were shut out of our houses of worship. Everything stopped. The people were very obedient and would not gather themselves together. All priests and ministers were sent to factories.

"Then two years ago, one church was reopened in each city. When they opened Tung Shan, people lined up over night to get the 800 seats in the sanctuary. There were 2,000 there for the first service. My Christian faith gave me purpose and examples to do good. Jesus washed his disciples' feet as a service to people, and this is the same goal that all people and governments should have—to serve the people."

Though Wood feels that in balance he has been very fortunate to be able to come here, he realizes that many others have been excluded. The U.S. has a history of poor dealings with China. In the 1860s and 1870s the Chinese were allowed to come with no restriction because they were desperately needed to build the American railroads and to mine American gold. Then in 1882 their labors were no longer required, and the Chinese Exclusion Act became law. It banned the immigration of all Chinese laborers for the next ten years even though the U.S. government had just signed a treaty in 1880 that said it could restrict but not prohibit Chinese immigration. After another exclusion law in 1894, Congress unilaterally prevented Chinese immigration until the 1920s when a limit of 105 entrants a year was established. The Chinese were virtually excluded from our western shores at the same time as Europeans were allowed to enter unchecked through our eastern harbors.

Only in this generation, after the passage of the Immigration and Nationality Act of 1952, could family members be brought together again in America. A 1976 amendment to the act raised eastern hemisphere immigration to 170,000, exceeding for the first time the allowance for the western hemisphere. This is the policy under which Wood Chuen Kwong and his family were allowed to come. And though he is a very recent immigrant, his understanding of and commitment to his new country is stronger than some who were born and have lived their whole lives here.

"The U.S. must be strong," said the grandson of a Chinese merchant in Vietnam. "The U.S. withdrawal from Vietnam and the resulting half million refugees may have helped to put the world in the uproar and turmoil that it is in right now. The U.S. has tied its own hands and is letting Iran and other nations beat it up. It is retreating to the point where it must now either surrender or fight back and move on. Compromise is not always necessary or best. China compromised with Japan and got overrun. Western nations compromised with Hitler and almost lost Europe, until they learned that one day they had to stand up and fight for what they believed."

Builder of the first steel plant in Canton, Wood girds the wide miles of his life and world with a song of strength from Feng Chih:

Man tempers steel, and steel tempers man:
Heroes of a new order emerge without stop.
For the many exemplars of man, I sing of Anshan steel.
What we do not understand we must learn.

CHAPTER 9

Hoa Ky Luu:

My Tho to San Francisco

Our births, our growth, and our sorrows
Are the lone pine standing on the mountain,
Are the dense fog blanketing a city.
We follow the blowing wind and the flowing water
To become the crisscrossing paths on the plain,
To become the lives of the travelers on the paths.

As Chinese poet Feng Chih found undergirding strength in steel, so he also saw the healing oneness, the Tao, of humanity with all of nature. His was a vision of family, of all forms of life, once separated, now coming together. His message is heard by both the Kwong family and the Luus who live just a few hills away in the same part of the fog-blanketed city of San Francisco. The Luus, like the Kwongs, are Chinese, but they come from a different country. They come from Vietnam.

Hoa Ky Luu ran the general store in the village of My Tho until he was drafted into the South Vietnamese Army in 1968. He was sent to the front but he did not lose his life. He did, however, lose his livelihood. In 1979 he took his wife and two young children and escaped the turbulence, confusion, and destruction of Vietnam. Thirteen members of the family, three generations of Luus, boarded two overcrowded boats and set out for Malaysia. In 1980 they made it to the United States. This is their story of sorrow and birth.

A Good Citizen

"You have been liberated," the loudspeaker boomed on May Day, 1975, at Cai Be Camp. "If you surrender peacefully, there will be no problem." Since their camp had been surrounded by the Viet Cong the night before, the South Vietnamese troops were waiting for orders from their superiors. All they heard was silence, until their captors announced victory. "From now on you will support the new government and not go back to what you were doing again. Now go home and be good citizens. We will call you for orientation."

"We were all interrogated," recalled Hoa Ky Luu, who ran the camp's commissary. "All the high officers and those who drew suspicion were immediately taken away and never heard from again." Ky and the others of low rank went home and were called to a reorientation camp nearby a few days later.

"When the communists took over, they confined us in one place with no freedom to go anywhere. I still felt that the war was necessary, that the United States Army did a lot of good until it withdrew. Most of us did not care for communism. When we were sent for brainwashing to their way of thinking, we were forced to do heavy labor, to clean the streets and to farm the land. And three times a day we had to go to lectures and listen to them talk about how bad the former government was and how good was Ho Chi Minh. They explained how bad the American government was and how we shouldn't do business with it.

"There were several hundred in my class. Then we were divided into small groups of fifteen where we each had to go against the American government and the former regime. We had to say all the right things that they wanted to hear. Almost everybody failed the first time, including me. They weren't satisfied with me after the first two weeks so they sent me back to the same place with the same group for the same routine.

"We had to repeat in our groups what they said in the lectures. We had to write pages and pages of confessions of what we did wrong. We had to say that we were ignorant before when we worked for the old government, but now we would work for the new one. Everybody wrote because we were afraid if we didn't we would be taken away. We had to give verbal confessions too. If we were wrong, they would correct us. If they found a real problem with what anyone said, that person was taken away and not seen again.

"After a month they sent us home for a second time. Those who had to go back for a third time were sent away. After a few weeks, they posted on an old army bulletin board in town the names of those who passed. I passed and I got a certificate saying I was a good citizen."

Out of Business

Good citizenship did not necessarily mean good business back in My Tho. Hoa Ky Luu and his wife Hoa Kim Chung were both children of small-town Chinese shopkeepers. Their parents were good friends, trading back and forth between each other.

"I went back to help my father for a few months." said Ky. "When I got back to business, the government said we had to sell everything at a lower price, as low as we could. If not, they would take us away. They had already taken all the rich merchants away for orientation, some of them for a year. When they came back they were entirely changed. They were skinny and afraid to eat or sleep. Whole persons were scattered and shaken. They had been put to work as field laborers and most were afraid to talk.

"We were told we had to pay more taxes—and retroactively back into the 1960s. If we didn't have enough money to pay them all, they would confiscate our assets and real estate. In 1978, our business and all our goods were taken. They also took one of our two houses, so the whole family moved into the one that remained.

"The people had no place to buy things, except from peddlers on the black market. The government officials sold back to the people the things they had taken from us. Everybody was unhappy and suffered after the takeover. Only those who still had money could afford to buy food, clothes, and other goods.

"Finally they sent us to In Hoa to work the land. We were able to buy about half an acre. We tried to learn as we went and we got help from others around us who knew how to farm. The government took all the money we had in the bank as payment on taxes. But we felt fortunate being just a few miles from home. Others were sent farther away."

At last their opportunity for escape came. Ky turned over two pounds of gold he had carefully hidden to buy passage on a boat for his two sisters, his wife and himself and their two children. The boat was packed with 227 other people when it set out on the South China Sea.

"We had some food, but it was vomited out on the rough sea. It was the monsoon season. The boat creaked and started to leak as we neared the beach in Malaysia. The water wasn't deep but the waves were strong. The battered boat slowly sank. Waves hit it, broke it, and swept it to shore. Some of the pieces never made it to the beach.

"The Chinese who were living there came out and gave us

food and clothing. Then we were taken to a camp at Bidong where 40,000 other refugees waited for a home. We had to gather our own wood and build our own hut, so fifteen of us built it together. There were twenty-four of us including children in that one-room hut for over a year. The six members of my family lived in a six-foot by six-foot corner.

"We lived on fish and rice, or rather, we lived on rice and lived for fish. Each person got one small portion of fish every ten days. Every second month we'd get a small bunch of vegetables and one chicken for ten people. There were fights for water and food, even murders."

As the crowds and chaos grew at Bidong, thirteen other members of the Luu family boarded a boat with 500 other evacuees from Vietnam. They arrived safely on the beach at Malaysia and lived off the food of the Chinese who were already there. But the Malay government, feeling overrun by both the Chinese refugees from Vietnam and its own Chinese minority, called a halt to any more arrivals. They put the most recent 500 refugees on five boats and towed them back to sea. One of these boats sank and Ky's father and two other relatives who were on it, were never found. The other ten family members finally made it to San Francisco a year later.

Birth and Renewal

"My mother, two sisters, brother, four children, two cousins, they are all in a four-bedroom place we found for them near here," Ky softly smiled. He was sitting on a folding chair next to a small sofa in the $325-a-month apartment he now calls home in America. Two other folding chairs, a pair of mattresses and a chest of drawers are the only other pieces of furniture in the spartan single-bedroom apartment. Just seven months after their arrival here, Ky and Kim move through their new surroundings with calm confidence and gratitude. Their five-month-old-son, Michael, the first U.S. citizen in the family, rocks on his mother's knee.

"Before we came, I was afraid, uncertain of what would happen, of what I could do. When we left we didn't know where we were going to end up. But I'm so happy to be here and I think part of the happiness I feel now comes because I found the care and fellowship of the church. In Vietnam, I had no religion. When they have to fill in the blank, most Vietnamese people will say Buddhist, but most of them have no religion. Here I feel that religion really helps and motivates.

Kim is similarly pleased with their sponsors, the Chinese Church and First Congregational Church. "The church has given me a wonderful welcome, especially in taking care of everything for the birth of Michael. There is an old Chinese custom to give out red eggs when a child is born. The church not only gave eggs, but also threw a beautiful party for his birth. I am very happy to be here. This has been a wonderful experience."

"I am so very grateful," Ky added. "America is a good —the best—place to live. I am happy here. But I think of my people back in Vietnam. Vietnam has much to learn from the United States. Here you have freedom of choice. I hope that someday Vietnam will have the same freedom. I hope that some day they will be able to have the faith I have found."

CHAPTER 10

Loan Vo Le:

Gem of Diamond Head

Fires spring up like dragon's teeth
At the standpoints of the universe:
A furious, acrid wind sweeps them toward us from all
    sides;
Aloof and beautiful, the mountains and rivers abide;
All around, the horizon burns with the color of death.
My parched eyes can shed no more tears.
In her breast, the heart of our mother shrivels
And fades like a dying flower. She bows her head,
The smooth black hair now threaded.
How many nights, night after night,
Has she coughed, wide awake, alone with her lamp,
Praying for the storm to end?*

    This verse and vision from Vietnam tells of the night of April
29, 1975, and the last flames of the fading government of

---

*From *The Cry of Vietnam* by Thich Nhat Hanh.

Nguyen Van Thieu. From Da Nang to Saigon, the bombs bursting in air—the dragon's teeth of civil war—destroyed a country.

Amid the shelling, rocket fire, and burning horizons, a woman lay in a Saigon hospital bed. She was alone, coughing, suffering from asthma. All around her, the horizon burned and people were running away. Loan Vo Le prayed for the storm of terror to end and for the strength to breathe and break through the enclosing fire.

Escape from Saigon

"I sneaked out at four o'clock in the morning despite the danger and the curfew," said Loan Vo Le. She left her husband Phuoc Le, her three daughters and her young son at home. "I felt like I would die if I didn't get to the hospital." Two days later, against her doctor's orders, she went home. "I decided that it would be better to die trying to escape than to die not trying."

Loan was a former American Field Service exchange student in upstate New York in 1960. Phuoc served in the Vietnamese Army Corp of Engineers. Neither of them had any problems getting U.S. travel documents. But when they went to the U.S. Embassy in Saigon on April 28, they were told that they were already too late for the emergency airlift.

"I went to my sister who lived by the harbor," Loan recalled. "On the armed forces radio we heard 'White Christmas' which was the signal that the U.S. fleet was waiting to pick us up. She told me that everyone had to pay $200 to get out of Saigon by boat. But we only had $20. So she took the boatman into her home because he had to hide during the day to make it look like he was not planning to leave. In payment he gave her six free passages on his boat. So Phuoc, our three daughters, my one-year-old son and I set out to meet the U.S. fleet.

"As soon as we left the dock, our motor started misfiring, so we sent out an SOS and waited and watched. I couldn't help but think of my parents. The night before, when the rocket shelling started, my father finally said he was ready to leave. Phuoc said we should split up if we had to, and then let God decide if we got back together. I said no, we must stay together. I could hardly stand up the day we left my parents behind, but I went on. I wanted so much for them to come with us, but Father went to work, although I begged him to come. I told him he was hurting Mother by staying, and that all my love will now go to her."

As the motor sputtered and they slowly moved away from the flames of Saigon, Loan Le looked down at her infant son and knew that the stomach infection he had had for days was more than just the flu. She went to the captain to ask for help. He quickly cabled for emergency rescue. The fleet sent a boat and rushed the Le family to the USS Kirk, a hospital ship reserved for women about to give birth and for those who were very ill.

By the time they reached the Kirk, the baby's infection had spread to his lungs and pneumonia set in. Everything possible was done, but the child died two days later and was buried at sea.

"We went on the Kirk to Subic Bay, the U.S. Naval station in the Philippines where all the Vietnamese were concentrated," Loan continued. "I immediately volunteered my services as an interpreter and nurse at the hospital there. The first day I saw a lady who was crying. I asked her why, and she told me that she was so stupid to leave her husband behind, because she had lost both her children on the way. Then I just burst into tears for the first time because it hadn't even been ten days since we buried our son at sea."

Sensing the need to move quickly away from the scenes of destruction and death, Phuoc signed his family up on a former gunboat that was going to Guam. After another week at sea, they arrived there safely. They stayed for thirty-five days. Phuoc worked in the camp's maintenance and Loan became a translator for the other refugees.

Kim Sa, their oldest daughter who was five at the time, grew up quickly in that spring of 1975. "Kim Sa used to come and feel my face in the nighttime, and know that I was crying. She asked me to try not to think of my son. She also made a pact with her father that they would not eat unless I ate equally. I had been skipping meals on the boat because there wasn't enough food to go around. All I asked for was as much water as I needed for my asthma.

"When the Kirk came to Guam, the crew gave us goodies. The Captain left us 100 pounds of steak. I wanted to share it with the others in the camp but the master sergeant took it before I had the chance. They offered money, but we refused. I never show my hand and ask for money. When they offered a car to take us around camp, I said no. I walked like everybody else and carried the children on my shoulders.

"I told our daughters that we couldn't promise them the wealth they had before, but we would do our best to give them the love they had before and the best education we could find. We had nothing left but my wedding ring and $10. We shared our tent with an engineer and a dentist and their five children.

"Five weeks later we were moved to Camp Pendleton in California. There the wife of the captain of the Kirk came to see us. She had been asked by the whole crew of the ship to tell us that they wanted to be our sponsors. But I had to tell her that I didn't want to be in San Diego. I didn't want to be that close to the ship. It would remind me too much of our passage and my son's death. My American Field Service family in Fayetteville, New York, also wanted to sponsor us, but I had to say no to them too because I knew it would be too cold there for us."

Coming Home in Hawaii

"We decided to go to Hawaii," said Loan. "I had stopped there for three days on my way back home from my school year in New York, in 1961. I knew we would like it there. The weather was like it was at home, and the people were casual and relaxed. At first living among the Orientals here made us more at ease. We were secure but penniless. We arrived in Honolulu on July 13, 1975. The Catholic Social Services paid for our plane fare. I remember that I was floating in my pants. I had shrunk from 110 pounds to 90 pounds, down to size five. But I only had an old size nine pair of pants to wear. I tied myself in with a string.

"Within two weeks Phuoc started working as a draftsman, his former job in Vietnam, for a man who was a friend of August Yee, our sponsor. He started at $750 a month, which was really big money to us." This good fortune aside, all the anxiety of the previous months finally came crashing down on Loan. She remembered her nephew, a South Vietnamese army officer who went home to his family one night. The next morning his head was found on a stick in the middle of the village.

"I was hospitalized for stress shortly after we arrived. I was released in September," said the former French teacher from Saigon. "At the end of October I started working part time in a Honolulu store. But six months later, the chain went bankrupt, so I entered a federal job-training program.

"After nine months there, the only job I could find was as a dishwasher at $3.70 an hour. At first they wouldn't give it to me because they thought I was overqualified. I insisted and took the job. After six months of dishes, they promoted me to a pantry worker, making salads and entrees."

And she began to eat. Now Loan laughs at the thought of how thin she was just a few years before. "When I was being treated for stress, the doctor said he would not release me until I gained ten pounds. Then it was a struggle to eat; now it's a struggle to stop gaining weight." Using her Vietnamese experience as both a flight attendant and a social worker, Loan then got a job with Aero America, flying refugees to the U.S.

"On one flight I noticed there were only women and children on board. I asked one of the women why. She cried and said, 'We were raped, some of us ten to fifteen times, in front of the children and husbands. Though our men begged the Thai pirates to do it away from them, they forced them to watch. Then they tied their hands and feet together and threw them in the sea.'

"When we go out for a picnic now, I still turn my back to the ocean. It makes me think of my son. For the first four years we were here I refused to go into the water. When I see the ocean I sometimes start to cry. But now I go to church by myself and there I can cry my soul out for as long as I want. I feel sorry for those who cannot talk about what is behind the tears. I once told the priest that I sometimes rebel against my faith. I look at my mother and father. They never raised their voice to anybody. They worked hard all their lives and now they are left behind with too little to eat. Why? Maybe God wanted my parents to bear the cross for something."

Though she is far from her parents, she grows closer to Phuoc by the day. "Phuoc is less hard on me now, on himself and on others. I push him and he slows me down. I believe in order. You need someone else to pull you along. He is the main pole on which our house stands. For a man of his age, he is very wise.

"Sometimes I get sad when I see how easy and secure I have it. Especially at holiday time. Christmas is the worst. I have to get the girls' presents before November because every December I get depressed. I start to cry when I compare what we have to most of the other refugees and the people back home. I usually go to the doctor for help when I feel down, and once he called Phuoc to come in and talk because he couldn't believe that we weren't having marriage trouble. I show my feelings, and even though Phuoc doesn't show it, he feels the same things I do. At least the doctor could see how good he is for me and how good we are together."

American Dream House

"I am proud of my start in life here," declared Phuoc as he walked through his partially built dream house. "We just bought this piece of land with my Japanese-American partner Hideo Kobayashi. He is like a brother to me. We met in Vietnam when he was on temporary duty for his engineering company. I work with him on remodeling projects here.

"When we finish this house in back, we will move into it, and then knock down the old one in front and build another new house there. Then we can sell them both and move onto something else. Right now I'm working for an interior design firm but I would like to get involved in art and architecture.

"Hawaii is a fine place for people who just want to relax. But there is more opportunity and better education on the mainland. In ten years I would like to be living in a suburb of a big American city and working as an architect and artist. I love America. I'd love to discover America. It's like many nations within a nation, each state with different laws and different people all speaking the same language. It amazes me everyday how you can talk about your President, about anything you don't like. In Vietnam, they would throw the book at you right away.

"I got in trouble in Vietnam for being against the war," he reflected. "Even among the students at our school I knew there was a net of informers. I was drafted for speaking out against the war. They made me an officer in the corps of engineers because of my civilian experience and sent me out to build bridges. We were assigned deserters to carry all the heavy material we used, and they were put under my command. One day we were working one mile from the village where one of the deserters lived. His father came out and kneeled down in front of me and begged me to let his son go see his mother because she was dying.

"I told him it was impossible, but then the old man tried to give me the one piece of security he had left in the world, his identification card, if I would let his son go. I was so touched that I sent a guard over with the deserter so he could see his dying mother. They both came back within three hours and no harm was done.

"But the next day, someone else escaped, and when I got back to my unit, I learned that the sergeant had sent in a report that said my leniency had let the other man escape. Some of the soldiers immediately thought I had taken a bribe from the family. It took a long time to be cleared from suspicion."

Phuoc lit a cigarette and reminisced, "I can't quit. I'm smoking 30 years of memories and friends. I know that to go back is only a dream. Vietnam will never be the same, the world has changed. But I miss everything, especially friends. I'm not really an immigrant, one who plans to go abroad. We are here because we had to leave. But the people of the United States should stop feeling guilty about the war. The war was all our faults, everybody's. The people from the voluntary services who came from the United States to Vietnam were the nicest people in the world.

"Anyone can invade another country. But God never allows us to exterminate a whole people. My mother, who is a Buddhist, says that we will pay for the suffering we inflict on others. We will have to pay with our blood for the blood of others. It disgusts me to see the communists in Vietnam now invading Thailand.

"I am grateful to be here and I don't want the local American people to think we are a burden. We are a shy people. We smile. We wait patiently. When we first came and didn't know the people here or the customs, we would send out our daughters to introduce themselves to the neighbors. When they came back with fruit from the neighbor's trees, we knew that here the people were friendly and willing to share. We have found a lot of love in America and we try to return the kindness. There is a Vietnamese custom that says whoever comes to your door at supper time is invited to stay and eat, no matter who comes, no matter how much you have prepared. Everything is set out in bowls, no separate plates, in the middle of the group, and everybody shares it all.

"When we left Vietnam I was afraid that nobody would take us. I thought that they might send all us refugees to some island or into the jungle. So when we got this welcome from America, I was really touched."

Loan is also thankful and knows that she has a responsibility to share the love she has received. "I thank God that nobody from our immediate families was killed in the war. I saw rockets hit other houses and only one baby survived. It bothers me that children here don't learn what Vietnam and the rest of the world are like. The children here also need to learn respect for those who are older. All of us have to be better. We must not live so selfishly. We arrive here and forget the people who are left behind, and the people who are just coming." Her 11-year-old daughter, Kim Sa, misses her grandfather, but has already forgotten the war.

Loan now shares her love and experience with the new Americans she is helping to resettle through her job as a counselor with the Hawaii State Immigration Services. "When I orient the new arrivals and they are slower than I am, I must be more patient and more soft on them than I have been. We all need to live more in peace."

Loan, whose name means "gem" in Vietnamese is now

well set near Diamond Head. She thinks often of Vietnam and wants to go back, but realizes that it is impossible. "If Vietnam were a free country, I would like to go back. I miss my family so much. But we couldn't stay. I'm afraid we are too spoiled by life here, the conveniences, the opportunities, the education and the freedom. In Vietnam we were always stopped for our identification. Here we are safe and free to move around as we like. Now Phuoc and I are applying for U.S. citizenship. Neither one of us would go back to Vietnam without it. I feel like a Vietnamese American," she said, pausing, "but inside I'm still Vietnamese."

CHAPTER 11

Somsy Kuamtou:

Lao in Kalihi

Here in the presence of the undisturbed stars,
In the invisible patterns of all people still alive on earth,
I feel like I am that bird which dies for the sake of its mate,
Dripping blood from its broken beak and crying out,
"Beware! Turn around to face your real enemies:
Ambition, violence, hatred greed.
If we kill, with whom shall we live then?"*

The borders of Southeast Asia bleed into each other. The battlefield stretches from Vietnam through Cambodia and into Laos. Death and destruction were the only constants that could be found. The people who were trapped as the armies cut across their land and lives had only two options: fight or flee.

In Laos, where the ethnic Lao were only the largest among thirty minorities, the Royal Lao government yielded to the communist Pathet Lao. Thousands upon thousands became refugees. Somsy Kuamtou, a Royal Lao, was one of them. This is his story from Vientianne to Kalihi.

*From *The Cry of Vietnam* by Thich Nhat Hanh.

157

Swimming the Mekong

Under the protection of darkness, hundreds of Laotians moved through the forest and came to the banks of the Mekong River. Somsy Kuamtou crouched beside the black water and waited. Bodies riddled with bullets floated by, killed trying to make the swim to Thailand. It was August 27, 1978, and he decided it was then or never.

"I slipped silently into the water and started to swim slowly and quietly," Somsy recalled. "It was a long way across the mile-wide Mekong, but I made it. As soon as I came up on the Thai side, I was caught by immigration and put in jail, but I was thankful to be out of Laos. If I had not left, maybe I'd be dead now.

"I stayed in jail for three days with a hundred people in a room so small that we had no room to sleep and only one bathroom. My brother came too. He had to stay in jail for six months. I was then held for ten days in a fenced in area with 2,000 others. There was one building, and it overflowed with people. So I had to sleep outside, even when it rained. Then I was sent to another camp close by where 35,000 people were packed into small apartments. I stayed with a man who swam the river with me, and I waited for the chance to bring over my family.

"I hired a man in the camp to bring my wife and children across for $400. He walked ten kilometers through the forest on the Lao side to get my wife. Then he gave the kids sleeping pills to keep them quiet, carried them back through the forest to the river where they boarded a boat for the Thai side. I got the money for him through a Thai bank near the camp. It came from my brother in Hawaii and my brother and sister-in-law in France.

"My wife Nhung, daughter Viengmany, sons Ut, Noy, and Be and I all stayed for fourteen months in half a room. We were given a supply of rice once a month from the Red Cross.

We got one coupon a month to buy meat, chicken and pork, but you could only get one meal for every two coupons. Once a week they gave us fish."

Though hungry and penniless, Somsy still preferred this to his fate in Laos. "In 1975, when the communists took over, I knew that among the three million people in Laos, only one in ten—maybe 300,000—were real communists. But they imposed all their rules on the general public. Since I had been one of the Royal Lao workers, a statistician in the Ministry of Urban Development, I knew that some day they would come and take me away.

"As soon as the Pathet Lao took over, they changed my position to treasurer and lowered my salary from 19,500 kip per month ($195) to 10,500 kip. Four thousand of that was immediately taken out for our rice ration each month.

"Nothing bad happened to me in the three years after the change in government, but I saw the Pathet Lao slowly taking away former Royal Lao workers to 'training camps.' They never came back. We never knew what happened to them. I saw people in my own ministry who worked too hard and tried to improve things taken away and replaced by Pathet Lao. I knew that my time was coming soon."

Safety at Last

Time passed slowly in the camp, but as Somsy explained, "Lao are a patient people." They waited, watched and listened while letters to families in Laos went unanswered. Sometimes they talked about the forbearance taught them in Theravada Buddhism. Merit is always more important than material gain. Pain is to be endured for the greater gain in the life to come. You are to be good in your life, not to seek the good life. The highest state is spiritual, not spatial. It is found not in this world but in the state of nirvana, a state of being known not for its boundaries, but for its boundless bliss.

In the camp, however, the only truth seemed to be the passing of time. The old people in the camp were near death waiting for release. One man had been waiting four years. For Somsy and his family, freedom came after fourteen months. "The American Council for Nationalities Services loaned us $1216 to fly the eight of us to Hawaii. We got here in October 1979 and stayed on the floor of my brother Kuammany's apartment. He had made it out before us."

For the last five years, Lao people have been coming to Hawaii. Many have already gone on to the mainland to rejoin relatives and pursue better employment. About 250 now live in Hawaii. Finding housing is difficult, especially for the large extended families Laos usually have. Sixty Lao families used to live in the twenty-story-high Kuhio Park Terrace housing project, but now only twenty remain. Living so high is unnatural for them, and the elevators, telephones, and kitchen appliances are more frightening than convenient.

One family who came from the rustic hills of Laos and ended up in one of these modern apartments was shown the oven range and told that it was the place they were supposed to cook. Later when neighbors smelled smoke, they entered to find the family happily cooking their evening meal on a roaring wood fire they had built on top of the stove.

Other aspects of the new culture they live in are much more threatening. The tall, boisterous Samoans easily intimidate these newcomers. The confrontations between the two groups are always one-sided and create an atmosphere of anxiety and confusion. The Laotians cannot understand why they are being bullied and have no real idea of what to do. Although someone tried to cut through his window screen during the night, Somsy insists he has no intention of leaving.

The sun is bright and warm by day. Chili pepper and peppermint plants fill the small garden that the Kuamtous grow in front of their neat, subsidized apartment. Inside, Nhung served a spicy sour fish sauce over rice. Other dishes were filled with fish, eggplant, cucumbers and papayas. "The food here is no problem," said Somsy. "We have more of some of the goods we like than we had in Laos. Language is the biggest problem, but we are learning."

Each morning, Somsy volunteers to help sort and pack the food and clothes that have been donated at a free store sponsored by the Kaumakapili Church. This church reflects the cultural mixture of the islands as a whole. Hawaiian, Samoan, Chinese, Filipino, Vietnamese, Korean, Portugese, Haole (white), Japanese, and now Lao all come to the church's health clinic and free store. "I like it here. I feel safe, I feel hope," Somsy said as he folded a small shirt and put it in a cardboard box marked 'boys'. "I have written to my parents once, but there was no answer. Some are afraid to write from here to their relatives in Laos. They think they might suffer because of our freedom. I don't write now either. If I do, the government will open it and my family will be in trouble."

Having said this, Somsy stood quietly for a moment, reflecting. Then he said, "I have shelter and clothes now and I feel happiness. But even though I lost my home and status in Laos, someday I hope I will be able to go back."

CHAPTER 12

Filipinas Amodo Sales:

Molave on Brown Legs

The glory hour will come.
Out of the silent dreaming,
From the seven-thousandfold silence
We shall emerge, saying: We are Filipinos,
And no longer be ashamed.

Sleep not in peace.
The dream is not yet fully carved.
Hard the wood, harder the blows.
Yet the molave will stand;
Yet the molave monument will rise,
And gods walk on brown legs.

The Philippines is an archipelago of seven thousand islands, seven languages, and fifty-seven dialects. Its first people came from Malaysia and China, but as the centuries passed, it has known Spanish occupation, American domination, and Japanese invasion. Christian and Moslem faiths coexist beside a profound reverence for the divinity of nature.

Within the islands, a stew of cultures and attitudes compete for influence and often clash, leaving many on the fringe of opportunity and power. Yet the people are proud and strong, not unlike the molave, their country's most durable tree. In the lines above from the poem "Like the Molave," Rafael Zulueta da Costa calls upon his fellow Filipinos to rise up and fulfill their dreams. Filipinas Sales did just that, but it required her to emigrate to Hawaii. It was there that her dream of a family reunited came true. This is their story, a family carved over a generation, standing together on strong brown legs.

A Two-Generation Dream

The family dream began in 1923 in Laoag Ilacos Norte. It was born in the mind of an eighteen-year-old fisherman. "I had an inspiration," said Pablo Amodo. "I wanted to go to Hawaii." He thought his dream would be fulfilled by the Hawaii Sugar Planters' Association.

When the Chinese Exclusion Act of 1900 and the Gentlemen's Agreement of 1907 shut off the supply of cheap labor from China and Japan, the growers turned to the recently annexed Philippines as a new source of workers. Filipino recruits were given fares to Honolulu and three-year contracts to work on the plantations. They were like residents without a nation, subject to the caprice of U.S. law. Attorney General John Matthewman, the legal overlord for the territory of Hawaii, said that imported Filipino laborers were "neither citizens nor aliens, since they came from a commonwealth governed by the United States." Because of this ambiguous status, the Filipinos effectively had no government to defend them at home or in Hawaii. Nevertheless, they came in large numbers. The plantation wages of two dollars a day lured them from the greater poverty in their homeland.

Pablo Amodo was a preacher. He was paid only ten pesos a month, about five dollars. He had to fish night and day to feed his children and his wife Martina. She too was a preacher, leaving each weekend to attend to her congregation. She too dreamed of a better life in Hawaii.

But Pablo was not part of the first wave of immigration to Hawaii. The long nights on the water, waiting until the nets held enough food for his family, had left him tired and sick. When he was examined for fitness to go to Hawaii, he exhibited the symptoms of tuberculosis and passage was denied. So the years passed and he continued casting his nets and preaching in his church. Christmases came and went. His children grew up and as he got older the nets grew heavier.

"When I had drawn enough for the family, I dragged the nets to shore, laid there and slept. Little Filipinas would come to take the catch and leave me food to eat. Sometimes we would sail 200 kilometers to the north in Cagayan, following the fish. Sometimes we would leave the wild sea and find the fish in the river."

Then in the 1930s the door to immigration was closed just as quickly as it had first been opened. In 1934 the Tydings-McDuffie Act suddenly limited Filipino immigration to an annual quota of fifty people. Sixty-five thousand men had gone from the Philippines to Hawaii by 1925, but just twenty short years later only a few could still be found in the plantation towns. The others had gone home when the jobs were cut off. But meanwhile, American citizens were allowed to enter the Philippines in any number and without restriction. By 1939, 9,000 Americans were living there and owning 63,000 acres of the land.

After the Second World War, liberation came and the Philippine Republic was born on July 4, 1946. Again, U.S. economic interests opened the door to immigration. The Hawaii Sugar Planters' Association and the Pineapple Growers' Association invoked Section Eight of the Tydings-

McDuffie Act that provided for exceptions based on labor needs. The lull in the current of hungry workers was over. Seven thousand arrived in 1946, most of them single men like Manuel Sales, Pablo's future son-in-law.

"Everybody wanted to go to Hawaii after the war," Manuel remembered. "We heard things about Hawaii, read books, and began to see people coming back to the Philippines in rich clothes, telling stories of how much they loved Hawaii. I was planting rice, beans, and corn for fifty cents a day when I heard they were getting forty-five cents an hour in Hawaii to pick pineapples." Shortly afterwards he came to Lanai, the Hawaiian island covered with pineapples.

"I worked on a pineapple plantation, living with a friend and an oldtimer who had been picking there since 1927. We joined a union, had a strike, and finally won a contract with a full range of worker benefits, health plan, pension, grievance procedure, and seniority. In 1950 I moved to Honolulu, worked in construction, then on four other jobs in one year, and finally went back to the pineapple fields. In 1952 I started working in a junkyard, taking cars apart. After three years of work, they gave me free transportation back to the Philippines, so I took a fifteen-day boat trip to Manila. I stayed, visiting relatives, for five months."

On the same boat was a couple from his church, the Full Gospel Tabernacle of the Filipino Firstborn. In Manila they invited him to dinner. There he met Filipinas Amodo who was the pastor of a small village church ten hours outside of the city. She was visiting her aunt and uncle who were the host and hostess.

"We gave our best," Pina remembered, "because we thought the highest of Hawaiian guests. When I was serving, my aunt pointed to me and said to Manuel, 'Hey, my friend, take a look at my niece, Pina. If you like her and are looking for someone to bring home to Hawaii, she would be a good catch.' "

"Two weeks later, Manuel and my aunt came to my house, but I was away at my church. A week later, my brother came to pick me up and told me that the family wanted me to talk to Manuel. The next day, in Filipino tradition, the relatives —my aunt and Manuel's brother-in-law—brought his proposal."

"Right away, I said no. I was wild. I was too young. In school I learned that you need a time of adjustment. He was thirty-eight and I was twenty-one. I had dreamed of going to the University of Manila, if I could earn the money. We were very poor. Then my aunt pushed. She said, 'You are the only hope, the only way for us to have a better life. Go with him, and then you can bring us all, the whole family, to Hawaii.'

"They guaranteed me that he was a good, God-fearing man and that a lot of other girls wanted him, but he wouldn't take them. He wanted me. So I went back to the field and prayed hard. I didn't know him and I didn't love him, and I wanted God to give me a sign. I was mad, frustrated, torn to pieces. But I didn't want to disobey and disappoint my family."

They were married at the beginning of the new year in 1956, two months after they had met. Two months later, Manuel went back to Hawaii, alone. "In 1957, I got sick," Manuel said. "They found I had an enlarged heart, so I went back to the Philippines. I couldn't even sleep. It was God that brought me back to health."

After two years together and the birth of James, the second son, Manuel and Pina again faced separation when Manuel went back to work in Hawaii. He immediately petitioned for his wife and family to come but it was rejected without explanation. In 1961, he tried again and this time was told that Pina had to write to the U.S. Embassy for a pardon. She had been charged with fraud and misrepresentation.

"In 1950," Pina explained, "my parents and aunt had borrowed a name for me to use when we were trying to come to Hawaii before. But the real person decided to come, and so there was a problem with her papers. I was only eleven at the time.

"I wrote the embassy and asked for the pardon. They investigated me, my husband in Honolulu, my village in the Philippines. There were many trips to Manila for questions and blood tests. Manuel had to come to the Philippines for the investigation. We would not give up. Finally I was cleared. But when I reached the United States I was afraid they would find out about my past and put me in jail. My English was so bad that I was even afraid to pick up the telephone. But now I believe the U.S. is really good. When I took my citizenship in 1966 I was free from my fears."

Family Reunion

Pina may have been free from her fears but she was also separated from her family. It took her more than two decades but she finally brought them back together. She got a boost from the twisting focus of U.S. immigration policy. In 1965, a new law abolished the old national quota system, and allowed up to 20,000 annual admissions from the Philippines. Pina immediately petitioned for her mother, who came in 1967. Then Pina petitioned for her father, four sisters and a brother all at one time. Her sisters and brother came in 1968 and her father was with them by 1969. Now the only family member who wasn't with the rest in Hawaii was Pina's oldest brother. He presented a different problem than the others. He had already immigrated to the United States, but had disappeared.

"My oldest brother came in 1946 to Hawaii. He wrote to us that he got married and was going to the mainland," Pina recalled. "Since 1960 we had had no communication from him. So when I got to Hawaii I wrote to Englewood, California, where we had an old address. But we couldn't find him.

When the rest of my brothers and sisters got here, we kept writing to the Red Cross and other agencies in various states. Then in 1977 we started praying about it and a miracle happened. Through Social Security, we traced his name to an address in Missouri. We called the whole family over to our house and started to fight. Some said we shouldn't call, that he wouldn't answer. Some said we should write. Some thought we should pitch in and send somebody there. Finally I said that I would make the decision. I said that we should take a risk and call.

"We were all huddled around the telephone. The landlord in Missouri answered, and we mentioned the name Amodo. There was no recognition and our hearts dropped. Then I mentioned my brother's name and the man said, 'Yes, he lives here. Just a minute.' When he came to the phone, I could hardly speak. His voice was weak, but it was him. I cried, 'Brother, we want you to come home.' "

They sent him a ticket and now, in their Waipahu duplex, he and his son have joined Manuel and Pina and their two sons to complete the family reunion. Pina's father and mother live close by and hold sway over their huge family of five daughters, three sons, twenty-six grandchildren and one greatgrandson.

Pina regularly prepares large feasts for the whole family and even for the four old ladies who live downstairs. "Since 1966, I have been taking care of my ladies," Pina said of her extended family. "I shop for them, cook for them, bathe them and wash their clothes. As a licensed Care Home Operator for the Hawaii Department of Health, I also attend workshops that help me with them and with my family, like the eight sessions I just finished on how to communicate. Sometimes I wonder how I do it, three meals a day, with inspections for sanitation, nutrition and safety. But I know, it's God and my family that keep me going."

The family also inspires its senior members. "I am

retiring," confided Pablo, but no one believes him. "I was sixty-two when I came here and went to work at a grocery fixing their carts. Then I worked as a janitor, dishwasher and a utility man at the airport. From 1973 until this year, I was the founding pastor of Da Filipino United Church of Waipahu. Now my son Ephraim will take over, and Martina and I will be babysitters."

Ephraim and his wife Jovita brought their thirteen children with them when they came from the Philippines in 1978 and 1979. Ephraim explained, "My parents came to visit us in the Philippines in 1975. They told us our life there was harder and invited us to come to Hawaii. They petitioned for me to come in 1977. That was the year most of our coffee crop died in the heat and the fighting between Christians and Moslems in Mindanao disrupted my theology study at Southern Christian College. After finishing my bachelor's degree in sacred literature at Davao Bible School, I took three children and left for Hawaii in January 1978. Jovita and the other children followed the next January."

When he arrived, the family was ready. He lived with his sisters. When Jovita and the other ten children arrived, his sisters and parents joined to buy him a house in nearby Waipahu. "Jovita and I had been teaching for nineteen years. I now teach at Lanakila and Liholiho elementary schools. On Wednesday night, I lead house services for our congregation, on Saturday I do home visitation and on Sunday I preach. I am also going to the University of Hawaii to get my master's degree in education, and then I would like to add a master's in theology."

"Everything is good for me here, only there are too many crowding my house," Pina smiles. "But I would be sad if nobody came."

The Amodo family is a large and happy one and their memories of life in the Philippines are similarly good. Though life was hard there, they seem reluctant to find fault with the way the islands are being governed by President Marcos. Not all Filipino families in Hawaii feel the same way.

Ben and Regina Junasa have a daughter and son, and an elegant home with a pool on a hill overlooking the Pacific. Ben is the director of the Hawaii State Immigrant Services. He is happy with his life in the United States and would like to welcome his parents to his new land. But though they have visited, their affections always take them back to the Philippines where they plan to stay.

Perhaps because his family and feelings are still divided between the two countries, Ben is sensitive to the relations between the U.S. and the Philippines. His opinions are not uncommon in the Filipino community in Hawaii. "President Marcos is the darling of U.S. business. American corporations really gained free reign and power with martial law. They bought up huge parcels of land, opening plantations and growing pineapples there and sending them here. They are perpetuating the colonial mentality and closing their eyes to the suffering of the Filipinos on their land. It is immoral for the United States to establish multinational corporations in a country where the people cannot own their own land. The church should be involved in issues of labor and social justice. Instead it has been captive of the plantation owners, here and in the Philippines. We need to take the lead from our Lord who liberates both the oppressed and the oppressor, who shows us how to take the stranger in and also to free the established powers to act with justice and generosity." Ben himself helps take the lead with the human services his office offers.

One recent Filipino immigrant told me that he was pressed by the Philippine consulate to retract a newspaper statement he had made that was critical of the Philippine government. "All I said was that among the reasons I left the Philippines was that employment was down and wages were stagnant. When Marcos declared martial law it was needed. It has served its purpose. The time is now overdue to go back to public rule." His car was vandalized. He did not retract his statement.

Yet most Filipino immigrants remain silent, holding no political views, or holding their tongues for fear of retaliation. "I could count on my fingers those who are here for political reasons or as former prisoners," said Nicanor Joaquin, a doctor whose modest second floor office is on old King Street in Honolulu. Some of his patients are Asians; some are Portuguese; most are Filipino. Many of them are the oldtimers who came to Hawaii to work the plantations in the 1920s.

"Many of these old-timers save money all their lives, living singly, working the fields, waiting for the chance to go home and claim a bride. Sometimes an old man retires and goes back to the Philippines to find a young bride and live out his deferred dream. He comes back to Hawaii with an eighteen-year-old girl and gives her everything he has. She begins to dress in designer clothes, gets a boyfriend, and the old man comes to see me in a state of depression. I try to listen and help because I believe in running my practice like a family. I give them a card with my home phone on it and people can call me in the middle of the night, but usually only if they have a real emergency."

Only in Hawaii for ten years, Nick holds deep sensitivity to Filipino ways. "I try to tell the old-timers with high blood pressure to lay off the bagoong, the salty fish staple of the daily Filipino diet. But they won't, so I just give them something to try and remove the excess salt from their bodies. In return, they bring me food from their kitchens, vegetables from their gardens and fruit from their trees. That's how they pay doctors in the Philippines, especially in the remote areas.

"There is a good intermix of cultures here. You can pick and choose, keeping the traditions that are the most constructive. But I think the saddest thing is the breakdown of families and the respect for elders. There are no babysitters or nursing homes in the Philippines. Families take care of their members and stay together. I saw a Filipino woman in a nursing home here and she said she would rather die than go on living there.

"There are other problems too. About 90 percent of the people in Manila are college educated. They are overcompensating for the time when the Spanish denied them education. Now they are overqualified for the immigrant job market."

So many of the old-timers that Joaquin talks about insist that the newer immigrants don't have a healthy perspective on their lives. These old-timers have suffered and sacrificed for what they have and they resent the newer arrivals who are educationally and professionally advantaged. This atmosphere breeds feelings of anxiety and distrust that are reflected in the younger members of the local families.

"A Filipino immigrant student was beaten by a local Filipino student in Waipahu and died," said Alma Balatico, a seven-year U.S. resident from the Philippines. She has recently been hired by the church-based Cosmopolitan Community Service Center to promote peace, understanding and cooperation within the Filipino community. "The new Filipinos arrive and go to school in good clothes and shined shoes and they are immediately ridiculed. It takes about two years for the kids to adjust."

"When I came here and got dressed in a tie to go to the bank," confided Alma's husband, Goldrino, "I was embarrassed because everyone else was in casual clothes. Here you can rub elbows and talk with your boss. In the Philippines, there is always a gap and some distance. Here you can argue, get your problems out and solve them. If it weren't for my experience with Americans here I might not speak so frankly," added Goldrino.

"In the Philippines, unlike here, if you hurt a person, that hurt remains inside. A grudge will never be forgotten. Now I can offer an apology to a fellow Filipino and feel free, even if the other person doesn't accept. Filipinos too often settle things by emotions, fists and knives. If we show that discussion is another way to get at their differences, then maybe we can change the way they act. The life of a new immigrant is hard here, regardless of what the old-timers think. Everybody needs some help."

"We also have to do family counseling," Alma added. "If the new immigrants want to have the right to petition for other relatives to come from the Philippines, they cannot be on any kind of welfare. No food stamps, no living in public housing. So many of them work two or three jobs to make it for themselves and their families here and in the Philippines. Then with the husband working three jobs the wife takes his absence as a kind of rejection and the real problems start from there."

Fortunately, no such misunderstanding afflicts the Sales and Amodo families. Instead of being driven apart, their new life in Hawaii has brought them closer together. Many of their dreams have been fulfilled and many more will be. They have become exactly what Filipino poet de Costa implored them to be: proud Filipinos, strong as a molave, like gods walking on brown legs in a new land.

CHAPTER 13

Sukie Uputuu Pouafe Abel:

Samoa Meets Missouri

Kaulana na pua o Hawaii
Kupaa mahope o ka aina
Hiki mai ka elele a ka lokoino
Palapala anunu me ka pakaha
Pane mai Hawaii nui a keawe
Kokua na hono a piilani

The people of Hawaii are renowned
For their firm stand in defending
Their land when the representatives
Of the enemy made every attempt
To bribe them.

These lines of Ellen Kekoaohiwaikalani Prendergast, whose name bears the mix of countries and cultures, tell of the fall of Hawaiian royalty. The song from which they came, "Kaulana na Pua O Hawaii—Famous are the Flowers," also speaks of the powers of the Hawaiian land, its stones and flowers, its offspring. The sense of things lost that pervades these words can touch all of us, especially the immigrant, who for better or worse has always surrendered something to the current flow of time and change of place.

Sukie Uputuu Pouafe Abel has given up the soft, green land of Samoa where she was born. As she stands on the concrete steps in front of her house of worship and looks across the street, she sees the old crumbling body shops and tenements that line King Street in Honolulu. This back door to paradise is downwind from the glitter around Diamond Head. This is where Sukie Uputuu Pouafe came when she married into America.

The Samoan Way

"Samoana, ala mai—Samoans, awake!" swelled the sound of the Samoan national anthem as it spilled from inside the church out onto King Street. Harmony ruled and soared. Within the church, women in full-length dresses as colorful as rainbows sang with their children. On the other side of the aisle, the men added the bass and tenor lines. They were dressed in American coats and ties with the Samoan lavalava cloths wrapped from waists to ankles.

Outside, on the steps, Sukie Abel stood and listened. A twenty-seven-year-old Samoan who has been in Hawaii for two years, she came from the village of Fasitootai on the island of Upolu and married a marine from the town of Prairieville, Missouri. In her meet fa'a Samoa—the Samoan way of life—and the American dream.

She lives in one of the long stark rows of poured concrete apartments in the Kuhio Valley housing project. But behind that drab facade, she, her husband Eugene, and her extended Samoan family have created a world of flourishing gardens, of fruit trees and flowers. There she recalls her childhood in Samoa.

"My father went blind, a complication of his diabetes, but he continued as pastor of the Congregational Church in Fasitootai. When he died in 1967, all five of us children were in school and my mother wasn't working. There were three terms of school each year and each one cost $20, so we had to do something to earn money in the month between terms.

"My two sisters and I took the seven-hour ferry ride from our island to Savaii, where my aunt had a store. She also had eleven kids. We would tend the kids and help in the store, cooking, washing dishes, weighing coconuts, whatever she needed. When we finished and had to go home for the next term, our aunt gave us new clothes and money for our school uniforms.

"The next term after we had visited my aunt on Savaii, we went to another aunt and uncle, working and weeding in their taro patch, and picking firewood and coconuts. Again we came home with full suitcases and fifteen to twenty dollars apiece. Then when we were going to school my mother, my sisters and brothers, and I lived with another aunt and uncle and their kids in one house. There were three adults and thirteen children, plus some cousins from rural areas who stayed and went to school during the week, and then went back to their villages on the weekends. On Sunday night they would return loaded down with baked fish and taro.

"During the week we would have a little fish cooked in soup with onions, curry and flour. The adults ate the fish, and we kids only got the broth, along with some baked taro, bananas, and breadfruit. One of us would climb the trees to get the fruit. We all helped each other because we knew our need and appreciated those who had helped us. All our relatives helped, even my aunt in New Zealand sent money."

When Suki left Western Samoa, she took with her the encouragement and gifts of the aiga—the extended family. Now her concern for the family and for others comes before

all. Before we were married, all her people came to see us, to talk and bring gifts. At the wedding they gave us Samoan fine mats and a wonderful feast. It's amazing how they can all get together, take the little bit that each one's got, and make it into a big banquet. I wanted my family to come but none of them did—not even my mother. I would have liked them to see the customs other than American and German, "said the marine whose great uncle shined the boots of Adolf Hitler.

"I've seen Australia, New Zealand, and the Philippines as well as Vietnam and Okinawa. But Hawaii is the best place I've been. This is the first place I've seen where everyone was friendly to me, and most of that's because of the Samoans. The Samoan family has got togetherness. If they have a black sheep or troublemaker, they don't show it. They can take anything and turn it into a celebration. When I first met them I liked them. They always have a good, easy time. I'm kind of shy and don't talk much, but these people just won't leave you alone. I'm a wallflower, but they brought me right down."

Nine years from now at the age of forty-two, Eugene can retire from the marines. Now he talks about visiting Samoa when he's finished. Until then he hopes he can stay in Hawaii and learn as much as possible about the Samoan way of life. "It's funny, my parents always wanted to forget about Germany," he said thoughfully, "even though my grandparents were born there. My parents would only speak English, and whenever any of us kids wanted to know what a word meant, our father would say, 'You want to talk German, then go to Germany and learn it.'

"But I think people need to know that there are other people in the world besides them. I envied the kids who grew up having to know another language, and to be able to speak it. I want our children to learn the language and customs of Samoa, including the most important thing. Samoans show respect: they respect everybody."

In parting, Sukie said with a smile on her face as she looked at the small, broken-down tenements of the other side of King Street, "It looks like home. The highest building in Western Samoa is a three-story Catholic hall. This sure isn't paradise and it sure isn't pretty, but people are great and it's a great place to be. I'm very grateful to be here. The land is beautiful and the people are friendly and free and generous. Here I want to stay and raise my children. They will be Samoan and American. They will be children of this land."

They will be their famous flowers—new strokes in the rainbow connection that spans this nation and globe. The kings are gone but the street still sings—for Sukie Uputuu Pouafe Abel and all those yet to come—the inviting and continuing chorus of Ellen Kekoaohiwaikalani Prendergast:

Kakoo mai kauai o mano
Pau pu me ke one o
    kakahihewa
Aole e kau e ka pulima
Maluna o ka pepa a ka
    enemi
Hoohui aina kuai hewa
I ka pono kiwila a o ke
    kanaka
Aole makaou e minamina
I ka puu kala a ke aupuni

Ua ola makou i ka pohaku
I ka ai kamahao a ka aina
Mahope makou a liliulani
A kau hou ia i ke kalaunu
Haina ia mai ana ka puana
No ka poe i aloha i ka aina

Hawaii, Maui, Kauai
Joined with Oahu in
    absolutely
Refusing the enemy's offer to
Sell their birthright for a
    mess
Of pottage. We the loyal
    sons
And daughters of Hawaii will
Exist by "eating stones"
The mystic food of our
    beloved land.
We stand firm in support of
Liliuokalani
Until she is restored
To her rightful throne.
Thus ends my song in honor
    of all those
Loyal to our beloved Hawaii.

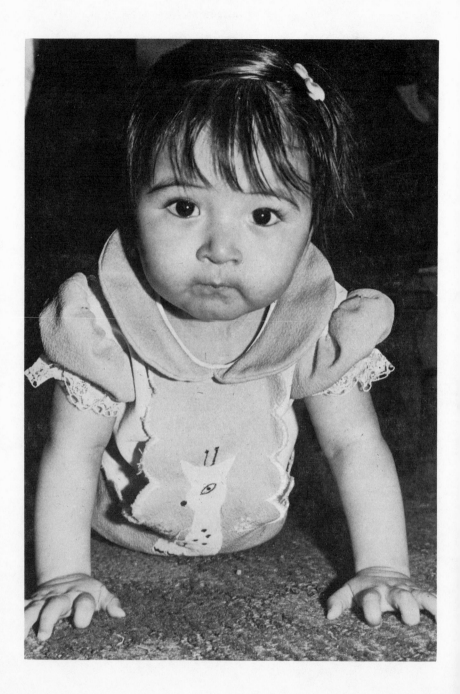

Projection:

Insurmountable Opportunities

We are confronted with insurmountable opportunities.
—Pogo

As Pogo goes, so goes the country. Confronted but not confounded, we are, as we have always been, a land of opportunity, a land of first and last resort. We were founded on an open frontier. Even our idols are portraits in passage: Washington crossing the Delaware, the Pilgrims crossing the Atlantic, the pioneers crossing the Mississippi. We are all heirs of the immigrant movement, but times are changing, the mills have slowed, the land is heavily taxed and water and gas are becoming scarce. Now, some of us are scared.

Problems of inflation and energy seem insurmountable. Opportunities seem to pass us by. In a land that is suddenly learning its limits, people who feel alienated from the rest of the world, perhaps from their own dreams, may want to close the door on others who want to come. Perhaps this is only temporary, a way to buy time and the chance to rediscover and revitalize our image. Yet doing so denies our own heritage. As Shakespeare said, "The problem is not in our stars, but in ourselves." It is not in the stranger, but all in the family. As Pogo knows, "We have seen the enemy, and it is us."

Immigrants have not depended on this nation as much as this nation has depended on immigrants. President Eisenhower called us "a nation of immigrants," and President Kennedy said we were "a nation of nations." So we remain. According to a six-year study by Harvard professor Oscar Handlin, there are 106 American ethnic groups and 173 independent American Indian nations. Our roots are traced to the oldest cultures on earth, including 150,000 Assyrians, 40,000 Egyptians, and 2,000 Zoroastrians.

Contrary to our fears of immigration draining our nation's economy, the truth is that immigrants infuse us with new life, giving more than they take. A study completed this year by economists T. Paul Schultz and Julian L. Simon for the Select Committee on Immigration and Refugee Policy revealed that new immigrants contribute more in taxes than they consume in public services. Within ten years after arriving in this country, they pass native-born citizens in earning power and their children overtake those born in the United States in academic achievement.

"The average immigrant is a remarkably good investment for taxpayers," Simon concluded. "They are not on welfare or unemployment rolls as the popular wisdon has it." Added Schultz, "We tend to attribute more problems to immigrant groups than is warranted from what we have seen in their rapid upward mobility in this society."

All the preceeding portraits and the hundreds of other new immigrants I encountered this year are living, breathing evidence of the benefits we derive from their presence in our communities and society. Along with them are thousands of others whose lives and achievements do not drain but sustain the American dream. One that I found in Hawaii is twelve-year-old Avion Vang. After living in America for just three years and having only three years of exposure to the English language, she won her elementary school spelling bee. She also placed first in math and second in writing. Each night she reads a book she borrows either from the library or a friend, helps her mother cook dinner and bathes her younger brothers and sisters.

Immigrants are not only interested in their own success. They also give us valuable lessons in responsible citizenship. In a Honolulu murder trial last year, all three key witnesses for the prosecution were immigrants. Eyewitness Sui Fong Ngai, a Hong Kong native, testified to what she saw when her boss was slain. The second witness, Zbysek Kocur, had fled Czechoslovakia in 1968. When deputy prosecutor Archibald Kaolulo thanked him, Kocur said, "For what? This is expected of me." And the third witness, Ahmed Rehman, a Pakistani, identified the gunman, after two men had approached him on his way into the courthouse foyer and told him to change his story. Rehman said, "That only made me more determined to testify."

In a nation where most citizens will watch crimes but do nothing to stop them, the courage and determination of this stranger is truly remarkable. As another foreigner, Alexander Pope, warned a century before we became a nation:

So perish all whose breast ne'er learned to glow
For others' good or melt at others' woe.

Strained Success

At the turn of this century, black activist W.E.B. Du Bois asked, "How much success is left in America?" This is a question we must all ask as we see real income going down and real unemployment going up. The cup no longer seems to be running over.

Americans, old and new, have always expected to make more. Now we are told to make do with less. But for most of us, the sacrifices we make, if we make them at all, will tend to be insignificant or illusory. Now as before, it will likely be the blacks, the oldest and the newest immigrants who will have to make do with the least. More than a quarter of our black families still live below the poverty line and black unemployment is twice the national average. The same poverty and lost opportunity that afflicts the blacks is shared throughout the reservations of our native Americans.

There is simply not enough wealth to go around. Anyone may be able to become a millionaire in this country, but everyone cannot. The climb of immigrants like Andrew Carnegie has always depended on someone else coming in, and staying, on the bottom of the ladder.

But now the bottom is becoming so crowded that there isn't enough room for everyone already there, much less for the millions of illegal residents moving over our borders each year. Jobs with a living wage should be provided for the U.S. born just as readily as they are offered to the new immigrants. If not, tensions will build to an explosive level. As Lawrence Fuchs, director of the Select Commission on Immigration and Refugee policy said, "There is widespread resentment against a policy that allows illegal immigration. There is anxiety, hostility, and outrage against a law that is out of control."

Short Arm of the Law

As the Select Commission and the Congress try to change this nation's outdated and outmaneuvered immigration policy, the legions of immigrants are still pouring through our back door. Immigration offices are hopelessly backlogged, and border patrols are helplessly underfunded and understaffed. "It is ironic," said Hamilton Fish Jr., the Republican head of the House Subcommittee on Immigration, "that we spend so much time on world-wide quotas and per-country limitations on the number of refugees to be admitted, and meanwhile the back door is open and as many people or more are coming in on their own initiative as are coming in legally through the Immigration and Naturalization Service."

We have even found official ways to avoid the letter of the law and let people in. In the last twenty-four years, Attorney Generals have used the office's discretionary parole power to admit more than a million refugees. Congress has made its own openings in specific cases, as with the Cubans and Haitians who landed, uninvited and undocumented, last year. But this action was in itself ex post facto and meaningless—the 150,000 refugees were already here.

Lawrence Fuchs is right—immigration is out of control. The law doesn't work. People do. As a result, people do such foolish things as keep large numbers of our own citizens on welfare and employ instead, at slave wages and in deplorable conditions, thousands upon thousands of desperate workers from south of the border.

The solution is not another fantasy-world formula that sets a quota here, or constructs a silly symbolic piece of fence there, as means of dealing with our problems. The borders with both Mexico and Canada are naturally and historically open and our immigration policy has to accept and reflect this. These two neighbors should have more access to this country than those from far away. We should either drop the national quota for Mexico and Canada or at least adapt them to the realistic needs we all share.

If the quotas are retained they should be projected for five- or ten-year periods, not for one year at a time as has so frequently been the practice. Our 1980 limit of 19,500 Cubans stands as the starkest indictment of our foolishness. Once these quotas have been set, they must be adhered to. Unlike the flow from Mexico, these 120,000 Cubans could have been stopped, but they weren't. And the reason that they weren't is because the Cubans are very attractive immigrants. Their predecessors have been a boon to the economy. They look, think and act like us. And they are foes of Castro and his communism, a sentiment that warms most of our hearts. It is, however, worth noting that the reception the Haitians received was much cooler. Is this because they were poor and black and uneducated? Apparently so.

Immigration has been, and remains, less a function of domestic policy than of foreign policy, less a service of the Justice Department than a service of the State Department. Better than planning for, or just accepting, another hundred thousand Cubans in the next decade, we should lift our trade embargo with Cuba and try to encourage a cooperative atmosphere between the two countries, wherein many of our mutual problems might be solved. We must also have at least as much consideration for the lives, safety and future of our Haitian refugees as we do for our Cubans. Cooperation and binational economic development should also direct our relations with Mexico.

Our military and economic support for oppressive regimes in Haiti, Chile, Korea, and the Philippines has contributed to the flow of people from those countries to ours. Aid and assistance should not be cut off to those countries, but it should be controlled and redirected from arms to economic development that would empower more of the people. We should oppose brutal, undemocratic, right-wing dictators with at least as much passion as we direct against communists. Now is the time to extend to other countries with communist or Third World perspectives the same positive model of material and cultural exchange that we have built with China.

The best protection against tidal waves of immigration is a foreign policy that breaks down the walls of fear and builds in their place the workings of peaceful exchange, of both products and people.

The best we can hope for from the new immigration law is that it lift the nationality limits, allowing larger countries and immediate neighbors greater access; continue the priority of immediate family reunification; grant amnesty for undocumented aliens who are living and working here; provide full rights and protection for all employees, and penalties for employers who fail to grant those rights; allow not only for "seed immigrants" with special talents and skills, but also for those with special needs that our nation might only, or best, meet; give preference to those who have been most discriminated against by past restrictions, such as Africans, Asians and South Americans; and incorporate refugees, with a generous and flexible allotment, in the new law.

In the past, worker identification cards have been proposed to limit the use of undocumented aliens, but counterfeiting is already so common with Social Security cards that this idea seems doomed to failure. There are also problems hidden within the desire to penalize those who hire illegal aliens. Three commissioners from the United States Commission on Civil Rights warned that such penalties "would have the undesired effect of causing employers to discriminate against easily identifiable minority groups whose members, though legally in the United States, might be mistaken for undocumented aliens."

In short, no law—old or new—can really control immigration, unless we sacrifice our fundamental commitment to protect individual rights and liberties. We must remain flexible. As long as the United States looks like the economic pie in the global sky, more people will want to come here to seek opportunity than we will be able to take.

People will continue to come with or without an invitation or the blessing of law. At its foundation, immigration law is always fragmentary. We live in an international arena and we must develop immigration policies that are formulated in this light. It would be foolish for us, in this country, to try to pass a law to limit the flow of traffic from New Jersey into New York. Similarly it is foolish to think that immigration issues can be confronted in some kind of vacuum instead of within the flowing fellowship of all the nations of the world.

The lines are already crossed, the borders already erased. There are more Puerto Ricans in the United States than there are in Puerto Rico. There are more Samoans here than there are in American Samoa. There are more Jews in America than there are in Israel.

As the Universal Declaration of Human Rights says, "Everyone has a right to recognition as a person before the law. Everyone has a right to leave any country, including his own, and to return to his country. Everyone has a right to a nationality. No one shall be arbitrarily deprived of his nationality, nor denied the right to change his nationality."

The preceeding portraits in passage introduced people who exercised their rights to leave their countries and change their nationalities. Some of them would not return. Some of them cannot. Some of them came out of an economic need or desire. For some, the drive was more political. All have arrived with a universal vision of a world beyond wars and without walls, secure and welcoming.

Uniting Faith

In many ways, these peoples' vision has been a fundamentally moral one. They come seeking a more inclusive human community. They come trying to make, out of this new frontier, something of a promised land. As such, they have sometimes been taken advantage of or abused. Occasionally reports surface of sects and churches that have virtually held lost and hungry immigrants hostage to their kind of beliefs, ignoring the real and desperate needs these people have.

Yet overwhelmingly, local congregations and synagogues, church-based community groups, and other religious agents have not only been clear, positive influences in individuals and families, but they are also often the only immediate and enduring helpers on the scene. Unquestionably, starvation instead of hunger would have been the lot of the desperate Haitians in Miami without the initial and continuing support of the church. Countless other thousands of new immigrants have been similarly helped by small and large congregations of religious people throughout the country. This kind of reaching out in faith to open the doors so a stranger can become a neighbor is a large part of these positive passages.

Haven on Earth

Most of those whose portraits have here been drawn for us faced disappointments when they awoke in this American dream land. So it must be. This is not the promised land, but a piece of real estate. It is not heaven, but a haven.

Here people of all great faiths remain in passage—to Nirvana, Mecca, Jerusalem or a city yet to come.

Here we know that we too are the children of aliens, who say with Moses, en route to the place where we will become one people: "A wandering Aramaean was my father; and he went down into Egypt and sojourned there, few in number; and there he became a nation, great, mighty, and populous (Deuteronomy 26:5)."

Along the way may be disappointment and bitterness, loss and exile: "Remember, O Lord, what has befallen us; behold, and see our disgrace! Our inheritance has been turned over to strangers, our homes to aliens (Lamentations 5:1-2)."

So of late our nation has tasted disgrace—held hostage by Iran, often alienated in a hostile world. Today we must decide again whether we will close our golden door and gate—or open our homes and share our inheritance with strangers.

In the same year that U.S. Senator Pat McCarran fought to keep our gates shut and won the passage of the restrictive Immigration and Nationality Act of 1952, Pope Pius XII released his *Exila Familia*, which began:

"The exile of Jesus, Mary and Joseph when they had to flee to Egypt in order to escape the rage of an impious king stands as an exemplar and a support for immigrants, exiles and pilgrims of all times and places who have had to leave their homes and loved ones out of fear of persecution or because of poverty moving on to foreign places."

Let us not now, out of the poverty of a vision lost, lock our door to the alien angels unaware. Our nation will never be fully prepared for their coming. They bear a dream that we first carried—that this nation be better than it is. We extend a welcome, and they extend the image of a whole new family.

We are called to bring more than what Massachusetts poet John Boyle O'Reilly called "organized charity, scrimped and iced, in the name of a cautious, statistical Christ."

We are blessed with insurmountable opportunities. We are the beneficiaries of an opulent land. We stand in a long procession of saints who all began as strangers. We continue to draw together the American family portrait. It is formed in the quest that the best is yet to be. It is framed in the question set by Pope Pius to the Senate Sub-Committee on Immigration: "Is the present immigration policy as liberal as the natural resources permit in a country so lavishly blessed by the Creator and as the challenging needs of other countries would seem to demand?"

U.S. Public Opinion on the Cuban and Haitian Immigrations

Do you feel the Cuban emigration is good for the United States because it shows widespread dissatisfaction with Castro's government, or do you feel it is bad for the United States because it is difficult and expensive to take in so many refugees?

Good 19%   Bad 59%   Both 13%   Don't know 9%

So far, 40,000 Cuban refugees have come into the United States, and 200,000 more may wish to come. How many more, if any, should the United States accept?

All or Most 13%   Some 12%   None 40%
Only those who have relatives in the U.S. 28%
Don't know 7%

Some people think the Cuban refugees should be permitted to settle where they want. Others think that every effort should be made to disperse them around the U.S. Which comes closest to your view?

Settle where they want	30%
Disperse around the U.S.	57%
Don't know	13%

Many Haitians have also been coming to the U.S. Some people feel that we should let them in as we have the Cubans. Others feel that we should not let them in because they are not political refugees. Which comes closest to your view?

Let them in	39%
Don't let them in	46%
Don't know	15%

U.S. Refugee Act of 1980

Enacted March 17, the new law:
• "declares the historic policy of the United States to respond to the urgent needs of persons subject to persecution in their homelands;"
• endorses "admission to this country of refugees of special humanitarian concern to the U.S.;"
• projects "comprehensive and uniform provisions for the resettlement of those admitted;"
• defines "refugee" as "any person unable or unwilling to return to " his or her country of origin "because of persecution or a well-founded fear of persecution on account of race, religion, nationality, membership in a particular social group, or political opinion" (this addition puts the U.S. in accord with the U.N. protocol and eliminates our prior preference for refugees from the Middle East and communist nations);

- sets an annual ceiling of 50,000 refugee admissions;
- empowers the President, after consultation with Congress, to admit additional refugees in case of "an unforeseen emergency" in a fixed number "justified by grave humanitarian concerns or the national interest," and
- requires the President, after consultation, to present each fiscal year a plan for the admission of refugees;
- establishes a director and Office of Refugee Resettlement in the Department of Health and Human Services, and
- authorizes $200 million annually for services to refugees.

Refugees in the World

**Refugees in the World
as of January 1, 1980**

Africa	4,045,200
Asia	7,292,500
Europe	229,750
Latin America	1,085,300
Middle East	3,312,500
World Total	15,965,250

Source: U.S. Committee for Refugees

Refugees in the U.S.

Cubans	665,050
Indochinese	260,400

Soviet Jews	30,000
Haitians	8,000
Romanians	4,850
Armenians	4,750
Poles	2,400
Hungarians	2,300
Chileans	1,300

Refugees to the U.S.
proposed admissions for 1980 from

Indochina	168,000
Other Asians	1,200
Soviet Union	33,000
Eastern Europe	5,000
Middle East	2,500
Cuba	19,500
Latin America	1,000
Africa	1,500
Asylum Adjustments	2,500
Total	234,200

Source: U.S. State Department

Legal Immigration to the United States, 1821-1977

1821-30	143,439
1831-40	599,125
1841-50	1,713,251
1851-60	2,598,214
1861-70	2,314,824
1871-80	2,812,191
1881-90	5,246,613
1891-1900	3,687,564
1901-10	8,795,386
1911-20	5,735,811
1921-30	4,107,209
1931-40	528,431
1941-50	1,035,039
1951-60	2,515,479
1961-70	3,321,677
1971-77	2,900,885

Refugee Services and Resources

Church World Service
475 Riverside Drive
New York, NY 10115

Haitian Refugee Project
110 Maryland Avenue N.E.
Washington, D.C. 20002

Hebrew Immigrant Aid Society
200 Park Avenue South
New York, NY 10003

Immigration and Naturalization Service
U.S. Department of Justice
425 Eye Street N.W.
Washington D.C. 20536

Immigration & Refugee Services
Lutheran Council in the USA
360 Park Avenue South
New York, NY 10010

Indochina Refugee Action Center
1025 15th Street N.W., Suite 600
Washington D.C. 20005

Joint Strategy and Action Commission
Taskforce on Immigration
330 Ellis Street, Room 413
San Francisco, CA 94102

The Select Commission
    on Immigration and Refugee Policy
New Executive Office Building
726 Jackson Place N.W.
Washington, D.C. 20506

United Nations High Commissioner for Refugees
Regional Office
U.N. Headquarters
New York, NY 10017

United States Catholic Conference
Migration and Refugee Services
1312 Massachusetts Avenue N.W.
Washington, D.C. 20005

United States Committee for Refugees
20 West 40th Street
New York, NY 10018

Washington Office on Latin America
110 Maryland Avenue N.E.
Washington, D.C. 20002

World Relief Refugee Services
Nat'l Association of Evangelicals
P.O. Box WRC
Nyack, NY 10966

U.S. Citizenship Petition Oath

I hereby declare, on oath, that I absolutely and entirely renounce and abjure all allegiance and fidelity to any foreign prince, potentate, state or sovereignty, of whom or which I have heretofore been a subject or citizen; that I will support and defend the Constitution and laws of the United States of America against all enemies, foreign and domestic; that I will bear true faith and allegiance to the same; that I will bear arms on behalf of the United States when required by law; that I will perform noncombatant service in the armed forces of the United States when required by the law; that I will perform work of national importance under civilian direction when required by the law; and that I take this obligation freely without any mental reservation or purpose of evasion; so help me God.

Acknowledgments

The publisher wishes to express appreciation for permission to reprint from the following copyrighted material.

The Saga of the Hokule'a, by Keli'i Tau'a (p. xv). Copyright © 1977 Melway Music. Reprinted by permission of Melway Music.

Traditional Spanish folk song, arranged by Joan Baez (p. 81). Copyright © 1977 Chandos, ASCAP. Used by permission.

"El Paso," by Marty Robbins (p. 63). Copyright © 1959 by Noma Music, Inc., Elvis Presley Music & Marty's Music, Inc. All rights administered by Unichappell Music, Inc. (Rightsong Music, Publisher). International copyright secured. All rights reserved. Used by permission.

"Recitation: Twelfth Canto," abridged from *The Heights of Macchu Picchu,* by Pablo Neruda (pp. 105-107). Reprinted by permission of Farrar, Straus & Giroux, Inc. Translation © 1966 by Nathaniel Tarn. Original Spanish reprinted by permission of Carmen Balcells, Agencia Literaria.

"Does Spring Come to Stolen Fields?" by Yi Samg-Hwa (p. 119). From *The Mentor Book of Modern Asian Literature,* ed., Dorothy Shriver (New York: The New American Library, Inc., 1969). First published by Beloit Poetry Journal, copyright © 1962. Reprinted by permission of Beloit Poetry Journal.

"Sonnet XVI" (p. 127) and "I Sing of Anshan Steel" (pp. 134 & 137), by Feng Chi, from *Twentieth Century Chinese Poetry,* translated and edited by Kai-Yu Hsu. Copyright © 1963 by Kai-Yu Hsu. Reprinted by permission of Doubleday & Company, Inc.

"Like the Molave," by R. Zulueta Da Costa (p. 163), from *The Mentor Book of Modern Asian Literature,* ed. Dorothy Shriver (New York: The New American Library, Inc., 1969). Used by permission of author.

"Famous are the Flowers," by Ellen Kekoaohiwaikalani Prendergast (pp. 177, 183). Used by permission of Eleanor and Mary Prendergast.